To:

From:

WALKING EACH OTHER HOME

A CAREGIVER'S DEVOTIONAL

ANN-MARIE MURRELL

Dedicated to Mom and Dad and Lisa; Jason, Mimi, Charlie and River; my biological father Jerry Bledsoe, and my dear MeeMaw who taught me how to read the Bible.

INTRODUCTION

While being a caregiver for my parents, my Bible and devotionals were constant companions. They offered inspiration and comfort at the end of challenging days, reminding me to "be still" and rest in God's word so I could start all over again the next day (or at 3 in the morning as was often the case). I write notes in my devotionals but after 5-6 years I've almost run out of white space. So I wanted to make sure this one had plenty of room for notes. It's good to see how far you've come, or sometimes how you survived impossible storms.

The 365 stories and anecdotes in this devotional were taken from my daily journals from 2017-2025. Even during the pandemic when things became extremely dark, God's light always shone through. Every day I strived to follow His footsteps, not my own, and in His time; that was the only way I survived intact.

Many of the days represented here were painful to write, having to revisit some of the most difficult journey of my life. But those caregiving years made me a stronger, better, and more courageous Christian than ever before. I learned to walk with God as I walked my mother and father 'Home' to Him.

I am saying a prayer for you, right now, that your caregiving years will be filled with joy and light, and that your hardest times will be eased and controlled by our Lord and Savior Jesus Christ.

(Unless otherwise noted I used the English Standard Version bible for scripture.

January

"And perhaps I will stay with you or even spend the winter, so that you may help me on my journey, wherever I go." **1 Corinthians 16:6**

January 1

"I'd rather be a servant in my father's house than a king in Damascus."
Corinthians 3:18

Don't you miss your life in Los Angeles?" That was a question I was often asked when I moved back "home" to East Texas to care for my parents. From the outside, my life in California was glamorous, easy. But living far from my family while they were suffering wasn't easy at all. As soon as I left everything behind and followed Jesus' lead, almost immediately my soul became calm. I was forever changed. Whatever I lost I regained tenfold when I learned the importance of the 5th Commandment: Honor your father and mother.

January 2

"If you wander off the road to the right or the left, you will hear His voice behind you saying, 'Here is the road. Follow it.'" **Isaiah 30:21**

I've never been able to drive anywhere new without some type of map or guidance system. But even after I've learned how to get there if I try to take a shortcut on my own, I'm lost. In college I missed a few turns outside of Dallas and ended up close to Oklahoma… And it's been the same in life. When I'm not sure what to do or how to proceed, if I don't turn to God for guidance I almost always end up on the wrong road. While I often question myself and my own abilities, I never doubt God's. When taking the time to stop and listen to His voice instead of mine, I never get lost. Every time.

January 3

"For now we see in a mirror dimly, but then face to face. Now I know in part; then I shall know fully, even as I have been fully known." **1 Corinthians 13:12**

When my parents were diagnosed with Alzheimer's we thought Mom's disease was worse than Dad's. She was always the quirkier of the two, so when she began telling us there was "something wrong with Pop" we assumed she was exaggerating. Just like trying to look into the 'mirror dimly', we didn't realize Dad was in the beginning phases of sundowning but because of her own disease my mother didn't know how to express it. Over time everything became clear, but it took patience and faith to get there.

January 4

"And let us not grow weary of doing good, for in due season we will reap, if we do not give up." **Galatians 6:9**

Some caregiving days were wonderful, but other days were absolutely brutal. Eventually I learned that the more difficult times were often internal, the result of not eating or sleeping enough and letting stress and worries get to me. At the end of days like that, I remedied with prayer, reading scripture, and talking to my sister, Lisa. I quickly learned the importance of keeping my own life as balanced as possible in every direction: diet, fresh air (aka 'breathing'), and a constant, unending dialogue with Jesus in prayer.

January 5

"And my God will supply every need of yours according to his riches in glory in Christ Jesus." **Philippians 4:19**

Prior to caregiving I was terrible with finances. If given a choice, I'd rather dig ditches than deal with numbers. But soon into my new life, I found myself managing five different bank accounts, for my parents and myself. At first it was daunting, but later I (almost) enjoyed it and looked at it as a challenge. There were many things I thought I couldn't do at first, but with the Creator of the Universe guiding me, how could I fail?

January 6

"Though he fall, he shall not be cast headlong, for the Lord upholds his hand." **Psalm 37:24**

When Mom and Dad were in Assisted Living together, Lisa and I thought it would be fun to get them a kitten for Christmas. But when I visited the next day I found the kitten closed up in the box I brought it in. It was fine, praise God, but it was definitely the worst gift in the history of Christmas to give to two people with dementia. They'd forgotten about the little guy and had wondered what the sound was coming from the bathroom… The entire drive home I prayed that God would stop me from beating myself up about it, and I also thanked Him for His grace (which ironically was the name of the kitten…).

January 7

"When the Spirit of truth comes, he will guide you into all the truth, for he will not speak on his own authority, but whatever he hears he will speak, and he will declare to you the things that are to come." **John 16:13**

Dad had been sundowning for a while now, but never as bad as when they were in Assisted Living. I was fielding dozens of calls a night from Mom saying he'd "packed his ride and left the room". I'd often find Dad parked on his electric scooter in a hallway somewhere, completely disoriented, confused, lost in every sense of the word. It was heartbreaking. Each time, I'd pray with Dad before guiding him back to the room, where he then faced Mom's confused wrath…

January 8

"And God is able to make all grace abound to you, so that having all sufficiency in all things at all times, you may abound in every good work." **2 Corinthians 9:8**

Sometimes caregiving is like an unending rollercoaster, but not in a fun way. What helped was learning how to pray continuously. I prayed before I spoke, I prayed while speaking, and I prayed while listening. And then I prayed when there was silence. Today the only way I continue to find balance and wisdom is through this type of continual, unceasing prayer.

January 9

"Have nothing to do with foolish, ignorant controversies; you know that they breed quarrels. And the Lord's servant must not be quarrelsome but kind to everyone, able to teach, patiently enduring evil," **2 Timothy 2:23-24**

Nothing, not even sundowning, was as difficult for me as the 'battle of the car keys'. You'd think the DMV would handle this when an elderly person is diagnosed with dementia, but they consider it a "family issue". Taking away my parent's car was by far the hardest thing I ever had to do as their daughter and caregiver. It was necessary not only for their safety but also anyone my mother would potentially crash into—but the arguments were brutal, and several times Mom even "reported me" to the Assisted Living manager or her nurse, claiming I'd stolen her car. (Right this moment I'm praying for any of you going through this!)

January 10

"And he said, "My presence will go with you, and I will give you rest."
Exodus 33:14

We were still under the belief that Mom's disease was progressing faster than Dad's. She was aggressive, arguing about the car, and calling dozens of times a day. Meanwhile Dad slept most of the afternoon with a washcloth over his eyes. We assumed he was tired of Mom but what we learned, too late, was that she wasn't the issue, it was him. Mom wasn't sleeping because he was awake all night, leaving the room, not knowing who she was. Even with God's guidance, there were so many signs that I still didn't know how to see…

January 11

"Wrath is cruel, anger is overwhelming, but who can stand before jealousy?" **Proverbs 27:4**

My mother was always the jealous type, but it came out full force in Assisted Living. She was especially intimidated by a lovely resident who mostly dressed in leopard print and flirted with Dad during their weekly Bingo games. I prayed hard for patience when Mom would inevitably make not-so-quiet comments about the leopard woman, who thankfully couldn't hear very well and, sadly, didn't have any family. When I'd point this out to Mom it always seemed to soften her heart. Temporarily. I pray for all of the people in nursing facilities every day, especially the ones left all alone.

January 12

"A man of many companions may come to ruin, but there is a friend who sticks closer than a brother." **Proverbs 18-24**

Countless times when I was caregiving, friends blessed our family with their homemade food. After an especially trying week, my friend Paula brought us a large pot of her Hamburger Soup; it was delicious and hearty and felt like the giant "hug" I needed to keep going. And Tina would often bring us food and desserts from her restaurant. God blessed us with a wonderful outside support team, with us to the very end and beyond. Having someone to pray with (and for) you will help more than almost anything else in your caregiving years.

January 13

"Do not be anxious about anything, but in everything by prayer and supplication with thanksgiving let your requests be made known to God.". **Philippians 4:6-7**

My parents had anxiety about everything from "the car" (that I stole) to doctor's appointments. They would panic the day before any scheduled event, worrying about what time they should get up, what to wear, when to eat breakfast...I prayed hard about how to help them with this and finally recognized they were the most calm and unstressed when they had nothing "planned" at all, good or bad. This meant keeping them home as much as possible, or rather out of "the car" which always made Mom mad. Even though their world became a little smaller, it was also less overwhelming and helped ease their anxieties.

January 14

"Know this, my beloved brothers: let every person be quick to hear, slow to speak, slow to anger;" **James 1:19**

You'd think it would have been a sad day when my parents forgot how to use their telephone. But at the time, Mom was using it as a weapon to call me day and night with accusations of stealing her car. It was a brutal period and the only thing that helped was prayer. What was interestingly sad was that after removing the phone, they immediately seemed to forget the entire concept of calling anyone in the first place. This realization led Lisa and me to cherish every moment with our parents, good and bad. Because they were fleeing, too fast.

January 15

"Trust in the Lord with all your heart, and do not lean on your own understanding." **Proverbs 3:5**

On a particularly difficult day (week, month…), I read in my devotional not to worry about the future because it is a 'phantom' meant to hurt you. That struck me hard because that's exactly what I was allowing to happen. Worrying about the scary 'what ifs' in life is like writing a ghost story in your head with all kinds of terrifying endings. As always, the solution was to give it all to Jesus and let Him handle whatever might (or might not) happen. It certainly made for much better sleeping.

January 16

"Be kind to one another, tenderhearted, forgiving one another, as God in Christ forgave you."
Ephesians 4:32

For many years my sister had been trying to take care of our parents on her own before I moved to Texas. She worked fulltime and was driving hours a day to help them so by the time I arrived the stress had taken a toll on her. Lisa and I had always been close and it was a blessing to be together taking care of our parents, but we've also seen families torn apart over caregiving. I pray whatever differences you might have that you find a way through Christ to resolve them; I promise, it will be worth it.

January 17

"For if someone does not know how to manage his own household, how will he care for God's church?"
1 Timothy 3:5

There's a strange part of me that loves cleaning and organizing. I enjoy the process of moving all the furniture out of a room, sweeping, mopping, dusting, even scrubbing the baseboards. So whenever my home starts looking too messy (or 'fur ball-y' from my cat), I know it's time to not only clean my house but to also do some intense praying. If the furballs are showing up on the outside, I know something's happening on my inside, too. How is your house looking today?

January 18

"I am reminded of your sincere faith, a faith that dwelt first in your grandmother Lois and your mother Eunice and now, I am sure, dwells in you as well" **2 Timothy 1:5**

During my caregiving years I often dreamed about my beloved grandmother, aka 'MeeMaw'. She was the strongest, most Jesus-loving Christian I've ever known, a wonderful mentor and encourager throughout my life. In those dreams, I would walk through her lovely house, exploring the rooms I knew so well. Everything was always so fresh and clean that I could almost smell it. Now that I'm a 'Nana' to my own two grandsons, my biggest prayer is that they will also want to "visit" me in their dreams someday when I've gone to Heaven. What a blessing!

January 19

"And God is able to make all grace abound to you, so that having all sufficiency in all things at all times, you may abound in every good work." **2 Corinthians 9:8**

It was a rough week with Mom. No longer using the telephone, she still knew how to send angry emails on her computer. In addition to being mad about not driving, she was now upset about not having control of their finances. For safety reasons they weren't supposed to keep cash in the facility, but they also didn't have anywhere to spend it. I understood their frustration; they were losing their freedom and independence. Worse, Mom never knew she had Alzheimer's and thought she was Dad's caregiver to the very end. So on and on I prayed, always for extra patience and grace. I would need a boatload...

January 20

"Good sense makes one slow to anger, and it is his glory to overlook an offense." **Proverbs 19:11**

Something was "off" with my parents at Assisted Living but I didn't realize what it was yet. Mom was raging too much, Dad was sleeping during the day, and nothing I did seemed to help. This was all new territory for me and as their daughter I prayed hard not to take anything personally and to be respectful and obedient, while dodging the bullets caused by their diseases. I prayed almost every waking moment but some days it was very hard to be around them at all, which only brough on guilt. So I prayed about that, too.

January 21

"When the righteous cry for help, the Lord hears and delivers them out of all their troubles. The Lord is near to the brokenhearted and saves the crushed in spirit. Many are the afflictions of the righteous, but the Lord delivers him out of them all. He keeps all his bones; not one of them is broken." **Psalm 34:17-20**

After my infusion for Multiple Sclerosis I ended up with a cruel combination of strep throat and bronchitis, followed by an MS attack that put me in the hospital. Through it all, even during my most painful hours, I found myself giving thanks to God that I was home in Texas and not in California anymore. I couldn't imagine being so far away from my family ever again. It took me a lifetime, and possibly my lowest, sickest point, to finally understand that nothing was more important than God and family. Nothing.

January 22

"But if anyone does not provide for his relatives, and especially for members of his household, he has denied the faith and is worse than an unbeliever." **1 Timothy 5:8**

Growing up in Texas we always lived near both sets of grandparents and they were huge influences in our lives. Unfortunately, living in California my son, Jason, never experienced this, other than brief visits home for Christmas. I thank God every day that soon after I moved back to Texas, Jason and his wife Mimi followed. It was a beautiful blessing that my son and his family would finally be a part in his grandparents' life for at least a little while longer. And praise God, my own grandsons will be a part of my life as long as He allows.

January 23

"Blessed are the people to whom such blessings fall! Blessed are the people whose God is the Lord!" **Psalm 144:15**

Weekend Bingo at Mom and Dad's facility was a dichotomy. It was one of the most fun times for them, but as an observer it was terribly sad. Lisa and I were often the only regular family members visiting so we grew to know and love some of the lonely residents. To make Bingo a little more dynamic for everyone, I brought bags of prizes from Dollar Tree: little stuffed animals, candy, door banners. I brought enough so that everyone could go home with at least two goodies, win or lose. I highly recommend doing this if you have family in a facility; it doesn't take much to bless them and help make their lives a little brighter.

January 24

"A joyful heart is good medicine, but a crushed spirit dries up the bones."
Proverbs 17:22

My parents loved Blue Bell ice cream, specifically Vanilla and Strawberry, possibly more than they loved me (certainly true on some days). Every night before bed they each had a large bowl with both flavors, topped with a vanilla cookie. For years they ate while watching the news, but near the end they became fans of Family Feud. At first I was concerned about this habit for health reasons; I prayed about it and my answer was that I couldn't take anything else they loved away from them. Lisa and I decided that as long as neither of them were diabetic we would continue supplying them with gallons of the stuff. We did everything possible to keep them happy, and Blue Bell ice cream certainly did that for them.

January 25

"For nothing is hidden that will not be made manifest, nor is anything secret that will not be known and come to light." **Luke 8:17**

Dad was becoming paranoid about people stealing his things. He didn't have anything of real value, but he began hiding trinkets in drawers and under his mattress: expired credit cards; pocketknives; tightly knotted socks full of quarters and dimes, a stash of his favorite soft peppermint candies. When visiting I often found Mom frantically searching for something Dad claimed was 'stolen'—a shaving razer, a comb. I'd sometimes pray with her to calm her down, then I'd quickly retrieve the object. Mom thought I was a genius for finding things, and I often wondered if Dad thought I was the thief...

January 26

"Rather, speaking the truth in love, we are to grow up in every way into him who is the head, into Christ," **Ephesians 4:15**

Mom had a doctor's appointment, something I dreaded because it involved driving. As always, as soon as I buckled her seatbelt she wanted to know why she couldn't drive. After talking in circles and making up my usual excuses, I pulled over, prayed aloud, and I finally told her the truth. "Mom, you have dementia." I told her. everything including how she failed the dementia test, how forgetful she'd become, all of it. For the first time, she seemed to understand. Her head was down and I thought she was crying but then she looked up and asked, "Why can't I drive?" What I learned that day was that truth, reason and logic were useless now. I took a deep breath and gave it back to God.

January 27

"For we all stumble in many ways. And if anyone does not stumble in what he says, he is a perfect man, able also to bridle his whole body."
James 3:2

Dad's sundowning was getting worse. He napped most of the day because he was up all night, and as a result Mom was exhausted and cranky but could never remember why. In hindsight, I wish I would have known what to look for and how to help both of them better. Even with daily visits I sometimes either overlooked or ignored what I later realized were very obvious signs. Through prayer and discernment, I began to question everything and everyone in the facility, including the "lower" employees (kitchen staff, maids). Unfortunately, sometimes management can't be trusted to give you the entire truthful picture.

January 28

"Every good gift and every perfect gift is from above, coming down from the Father of lights, with whom there is no variation or shadow due to change." **James 1:17**

My parents were in such a great mood that I bravely suggested a car trip to Andy's Custard. Dad, completely deadpan, said, "I'd kill for it." I laughed hard and he barely cracked a smile, very much like the old dad. And for the first time in months, there were no arguments about cars or driving, we all just enjoyed our delicious frozen custards. When we finished, Dad insisted we save the cups because they were a "very high-quality material". It was a blessed day and I praised God through every moment.

January 29

"(For every house is built by someone, but the builder of all things is God.)" **Hebrews 3:4**

Dad designed and built one of the only underground houses in East Texas. All was fine until he wasn't able to keep up with repairs, resulting in extensive damage. I did the best I could to remodel and fix everything in order to sell it, but other than Dad, few people knew how to repair water seepage in an underground house. After spending a frustrating year in prayer about our family home, the perfect couple fell in love with it. Not only did they know how to make the needed repairs but they also kept Dad's original design intact. By then, both parents had long forgotten everything about the house, but they would have loved knowing it was in such good hands.

January 30

"When you pass through the waters, I will be with you; and through the rivers, they shall not overwhelm you; when you walk through fire you shall not be burned, and the flame shall not consume you." **Isaiah 43:2**

Mom and I were sitting in rockers on the facility porch and all was well until it turned into a huge circle-talk about the usual bad things. I tried to talk reasonably, changed the subject, and was finally able to leave on what I thought was a good note. But when home I had an email from her about how I'd always loved my dead biological father more than her...As I prayed that night I realized that even with much of her mind gone, Mom still had the same holes in her heart that she'd carried with her from her childhood (and mine). Once I finally recognized this, I said prayers of gratitude because her words could never hurt me again.

January 31

"Thou shall not steal." **Exodus 20:15**

I was spending a rare weekend with my 'Honeybee' friends Paula, Amy, and Betsy. We played a Q&A game and my question was, 'If you accidentally brought something home from a store that you didn't pay for, would you return it?" All three of them said 'yes' but I hesitated and made several excuses why I might keep it. They jumped all over me. "You do what's right and take it back!' Betsy yelled, and we had a big laugh. Next morning, I felt something hard in the toe of my new rain boot. I reached in and found...a new eyeshadow. Had someone meant to steal it and tucked it inside the boot? Who knows, but there it was, in my hand. I looked up at the sky laughing and said, "Okay Lord, another blatant lesson learned." (And yes, I took it back to the store!)

February

"So we have come to know and believe the love that God has for us. God is love, and whoever abides in love abides in God, and God abides in him." **1 John 4:16**

February 1

"So to keep me from becoming conceited…a thorn was given me in the flesh, a messenger of Satan to harass me, to keep me from becoming conceited. Three times I pleaded with the Lord about this, that it should leave me. But he said to me, "My grace is sufficient for you, for my power is made perfect in weakness." **2 Corinthians 12:7-10**

Dad's disease was progressing much faster than Mom's, and my own disease, Multiple Sclerosis, was getting bad, too. I was in constant pain so I only stayed with them a few hours every day. This meant Mom was stuck day and night with a man whose disease was causing him to slowly lose his mind. But because of her own disease, she took Dad's actions personally, as an afront to her. She didn't know how to separate her husband, "Gene", from his disease. The most and best I could do at the time was pray. And I did, on my knees. With a heating pad…

February 2

"But let each one test his own work, and then his reason to boast will be in himself alone and not in his neighbor." **Galatians 6:4**

My daughter-in-law Mimi loved Bingo possibly more than anyone in Assisted Living. She played with us as often as possible and to say she was 'very competitive' is an understatement. The problem, however, was that the older folks liked to win Bingo, too. On one particularly lucky streak, Mimi had already won twice in a row and was about to call out "BINGO!" a third time until I nudged her and shook my head 'no'. I'm not sure I've ever seen a more disappointed look on her face, then or since. I was proud of her for holding back, but if you ask her today, I'm pretty sure she'll still claim all 3 victories. (Happy Birthday, Mimi, God blessed us all when you came into our lives!)

February 3

"In all things I have shown you that by working hard in this way we must help the weak and remember the words of the Lord Jesus, how he himself said, 'It is more blessed to give than to receive.'" **Acts 20:35**

On their final day in Assisted Living, Dad drove his electric scooter straight into Mom's. I yelled out "STOP!' but he was in a complete fog. I started to panic but Mom calmly walked over, turned off the key, and helped Dad off the scooter. She walked him to his chair and covered him with blankets. I prayed, thanking God for such grace. Before falling asleep Dad slurred, "I need to go outside to smoke a cigarette." I was glad Mom didn't hear that; they both quit smoking decades ago. I will always remember this moment and the way Mom showed such care for Dad, because it was the last time I'd ever see my parents together again.

February 4

"And he awoke and rebuked the wind and said to the sea, "Peace! Be still!" And the wind ceased, and there was a great calm." **Mark 4:39**

For two weeks in 2020 my father had to be placed in a psychiatric hospital. He was detoxing after being overmedicated by Assisted Living, which resulted in him becoming violent towards Mom. Lisa and I had to hurriedly move our frightened mother into my apartment; it was traumatizing for all of us. After this day, the only way I survived and became stronger than ever was through my relationship with Jesus Christ. He carried me when I had no idea how I could take even one more step. He lifted me high above the rough waters and steadied my hand when all I could do was shake in fear. Thank you, Jesus. Amen.

February 5

"Be patient, therefore, brothers, until the coming of the Lord. See how the farmer waits for the precious fruit of the earth, being patient about it, until it receives the early and the late rains." **James 5:7**

Mom and I were in the doctor's waiting room. With all the stress and changes, I was pretty sure she had a UTI; she hadn't been sleeping and was acting very strange. While reading a magazine she suddenly looked up and announced loudly, "I just want to scream!" Later in the exam room I tried to make sure everyone only addressed Mom but she still said, several times, "I'm the patient, why isn't anyone talking to me?" And then my heart broke for her; I had to pray for extra kindness after Mom asked a nurse what type of teaching position she was interviewing for...My poor mother was so lost. And yes, she did have a raging UTI.

February 6

"The Lord will fight for you, and you have only to be silent." **Exodus 14:14**

While packing up my parent's Assisted Living apartment I found formerly "lost" items that Dad had tucked under his mattress: 2 unopened bottles of Brut cologne, a package of his favorite soft peppermint candies, and the funny Japanese bank from Amazon that Dad claimed was an 'heirloom' from his mother. Later when Mom saw us bringing in some of their furniture and boxes she broke down, crying and confused to see things that belonged to her and Dad, only he was gone. I prayed for help. Just then, Mimi ran in to tell us there was a hot air balloon hovering over the complex. Mom went out to see; she smiled and clapped. I thanked God for His perfect timing and continuous help.

February 7

"Rejoice in hope, be patient in tribulation, be constant in prayer."
Romans 12:12

Dad was now in Memory Care and I was having issues with his hospice nurses. Several times I got phone calls from them and instead of talking to me first, they'd put Dad on the phone and he'd beg me to take him home or ask where his mother was. Mom was always sitting right next to me, paranoid when I spoke on the phone. So I'd step outside and tearfully do my best to try to pacify my father. And then after praying for God to take away my anger, I'd call the nurse back and explain why she couldn't do that to me (or Mom) anymore. During those early days I believe God was training me in patience; I would certainly need lots of it in the years to come.

February 8

"The Lord is near to the brokenhearted and saves the crushed in spirit."
Psalm 34:18

In addition to everything I was experiencing with my parents, I was also having to tie up loose ends in California. Sometimes I was incredibly lonely, missing the people I had to leave behind. But through the darkest times, with my parent's advancing Alzheimer's and my own worsening MS, I learned to offer up prayers of gratitude regardless of my situation. I was honored to be a caregiver, and even though I still had grief for all I lost in California, I gained so much more in my simple but blessed life in East Texas.

February 9

"Casting all your anxieties on him, because he cares for you." **1 Peter: 5-7**

Dad was wandering in Memory Care day and night, often without his walker. This was especially odd, considering for the last decade he wouldn't even walk to the bathroom without help because he was terrified of falling. Now, he was walking like Forrest Gump, his feet severely swollen because they were never elevated. He slept on the lobby couch or wherever he could find a place to pass out. My heart ached for him, but I was tied up with Mom and couldn't be with him enough. I had to trust that between the facility nurses and his hospice team he would be taken care. And I prayed for him, almost every moment of the day.

February 10

"Rejoice in the Lord always; again I will say, rejoice." **Philippians 4:4**

Prior to moving to Assisted Living Mom never wanted to leave Dad alone but when he began sundowning she wanted to get away. Normally I did all their grocery shopping alone but this time I brought her with me to Walmart, and what a blessing! From the moment we entered the store she was absolutely giddy. Mom wanted to walk down every aisle in the entire store, putting random items in the cart. She talked to everyone she saw, hugged people and kissed babies (something she couldn't do when Covid hit). Disneyland wouldn't have been as much fun for my mother as Walmart was that day. Before going to sleep, I prayed immense gratitude. Tomorrow might be rough again but today was absolutely lovely.

February 11

"Finally, brothers, whatever is true, whatever is honorable, whatever is just, whatever is pure, whatever is lovely, whatever is commendable, if there is any excellence, if there is anything worthy of praise, think about these things." **Philippians 4:8**

Mom and I loved doing jigsaw puzzles together. Eventually I was only getting us simple collage-style puzzles, putting together a 'skeleton' outline, and sorting all of the pieces for each separate smaller puzzle within. It took time and patience but was worth it, being able to continue puzzling with Mom almost to the end. I thank God for those puzzles because it gave me time during such a chaotic, stressful season of life to BE STILL and pray while also enjoying peaceful hours with my mother.

February 12

"And let us consider how to stir up one another to love and good works, not neglecting to meet together, as is the habit of some, but encouraging one another, and all the more as you see the Day drawing near."
Hebrews 10:24-25

So many times after praying for discernment I needed additional 'wise counsel' from friends. Whether it was advice about something medical, spiritual, or just the need to vent and cry, I could call on a variety of 'counselors' who wouldn't simply commiserate but who knew how to advise and pray in the right direction. I thank God, daily, for these wonderful friends and I pray all of you have a team ready to help you, too. (And remember: They won't know how or when to help until you ask.)

February 13

"And Abraham went quickly into the tent to Sarah and said, "Quick! Three seahs of fine flour! Knead it and make cakes." **Genesis 18:6**

If asked, Mom would say her favorite meal was "dessert". We were blessed to have friends who appreciated her appetite for all-things sugar, like Tina with bags full of cookies and cakes from her bakery, or Mary Wallace's famous pound cake. Thankfully she never had diabetes, so I let her eat as many sweet treats as she wanted. Even near the end, I'd hear her stirring in her room, digging in drawers looking for cookies. Sometimes the answers to our prayers are the simplest things, even if it's just a cookie or two.

February 14

"Since therefore Christ suffered in the flesh, arm yourselves with the same way of thinking, for whoever has suffered in the flesh has ceased from sin,"
1 Peter 4:1

Once my parents had to be separated their long-time nurse advised us not to let Mom visit Dad in Memory Care. It would be too confusing for both of them and each time she left it would be devastating. This was heartbreaking. Mom and Dad had been happily married almost 53 years but the combination of their diseases proved toxic and ultimately dangerous for Mom. In the beginning I showed her videos of Dad in Memory Care, thinking it might help. It didn't. We realized in Mom's mind he was already gone, and Dad "lost" her long before they were separated. In a way, it was a lovely cushion of God's grace that they simply, sadly, forgot each other...

February 15

"But if we walk in the light, as he is in the light, we have fellowship with one another, and the blood of Jesus his Son cleanses us from all sin." **1 John: 1:7**

I tried to take Mom to various churches in town but there were always issues. Either they didn't have hearing devices and she couldn't hear, or they were overwhelmingly large and loud. Ultimately my 'wise counsel' friend, Betsy, reminded me that my mother's salvation was settled; she had been a regular church attendee her entire life. She sang in the choir, taught Sunday school, and was even studying to become a Lay Minister. Mom and I prayed together every night until the very end. Yes, Jesus loved my mother, church or not.

February 16

"She opens her mouth with wisdom, and the teaching of kindness is on her tongue." **Proverbs 31:26**

One of my hardest lessons was to never argue with dementia, no matter how absurd. The unofficial rules are that you are supposed to just agree and let them live in their "crazy". This is difficult because as Christians we aren't supposed to lie, especially to our parents. But when their 85-year-old minds ask questions like, "Is my daddy coming home?" it's better to say, "He's at home resting" than to repeatedly kill their beloved family member over and over. They will move on to other things quicker if you appease or change the subject instead of trying to reason; with Alzheimer's and dementia, the days of rational thinking are over.

February 17

"Peace I leave with you; my peace I give to you. Not as the world gives do I give to you. Let not your hearts be troubled, neither let them be afraid."
John 14:27

One evening Mom told Lisa and me that she wanted to give us something. She went to her room and came back with her and Dad's wedding bands. She said she didn't want to wear it anymore and wanted us to have them now. We didn't want to ask any questions, but I told her, "We'll be happy to keep these for you for now. Maybe when things are better, you'll want to wear yours again." Lisa and I hugged her. Our mama was sad and grieving and couldn't fully understand why. I prayed she could be happy again someday...

February 18

"For from his fullness we have all received, grace upon grace." **John 1:16**

Lisa and Dad had always been especially close, so it was very difficult for her to visit him when he began seriously declining. Sometimes he could be very cruel; he once called Lisa a horrible name because she wouldn't take him home. She broke down for days over it, unable to separate Dad from his illness. Other times his indifference hurt Lisa just as much. But one day she called to say she had a happy visit on her lunch break. "He offered me his ice cream cup, telling me, 'Everything here is free!'" We were finally able to laugh a little, grateful that our father had an afternoon of grace. And free ice cream.

February 19

"Not only that, but we rejoice in our sufferings, knowing that suffering produces endurance, and endurance produces character, and character produces hope," **Romans 5:3-4**

It was 2020 and Mom was in the ER with a back spasm. We had to wait almost 10 hours before getting a room because the new "Coronavirus" was spreading around the world. At the same time, hospice called to tell me Dad was on the verge of getting kicked out Memory Care unless they heavily medicated him. He was becoming a danger to himself and others. Overwhelmed, I prayed for Jesus to help me and at that moment my friend Amy Nelson walked up. We talked and prayed about it, then I gave hospice the go-ahead. And I thanked God for sending wise counsel when I needed it.

February 20

"And when the Pharisees saw this, they said to his disciples, "Why does your teacher eat with tax collectors and sinners?" But when he heard it, he said, "Those who are well have no need of a physician, but those who are sick." **Matthew 9:11-12**

Pastor Thomas McCracken from CommUnity Church in Virginia once spoke about his youth and how he was rejected by both his father and stepfather. Several members of my family could relate to this and in many ways, I could, too. Pastor Tom said he was finally reconciled through Matthew 12:15. *"If Jesus accepts us, what more could we ever need?"* On May 19, 2024, Pastor Tom baptized me in a river near his church. Praise Jesus for His ultimate healing.

February 21

"Think over what I say, for the Lord will give you understanding in everything." **2 Timothy: 2:7**

Mom was taking strong antibiotics and was very confused all night and morning. She seemed frightened, continually asking where she was and why she was here. I helped brush her teeth and put in her hearing aids and glasses to give her better perspective. I asked if she knew who I was and she only repeated, "Who I am" over and over. I was crying and praying while making her breakfast when she came up to me smiling and said, "You're Ann Marie, you're my baby". She was calm, happy. I hugged her, thanking God for clearing her mind and then prayed that He would calm me down now, too...

February 22

"For this reason I bow my knees before the Father, from whom every family in heaven and on earth is named" **Ephesians 3:14-14**

Lisa came over to watch a movie with us. It was fun being together, leaving our troubles behind us for a while. After the movie I was getting ready for bed when Mom knocked on my door. She looked concerned and asked, "Would it be okay if I keep living here with you?" I hugged her tight and told her, "Of course, Mama, you'll be here forever!" She was crying; her confusion of moving was passing. After taking her back to her room we prayed, thanking God for bringing our family together.

February 23

"Anxiety in a man's heart weighs him down, but a good word makes him glad." **Proverbs 12:25**

While Dad was repeatedly falling down in Memory Care, Mom had her first fall in my apartment. She was fine but now terrified of falling again. A physical therapist came over to teach both of us how to get her up from the floor if/when she fell again. As he lowered Mom to her knees, she panicked and began crying out for help. The only way I could get her to calm down was by holding her face in my hands and telling her to look me in the eyes. Talking to her like a child, assuring her she was going to be fine. "Breathe and pray, Mom," I said. She settled down, but from that day on she never took another step without her cane.

February 24

"And he said to him, "Truly, I say to you, today you will be with me in paradise." **Luke 23:43**

I never knew much about hospice until my Aunt Elvera was dying (on this day in 2019). Confused, I asked my cousin Preston, "Where's her IV? Where's the doctor?" It was amazing how calm he was as he explained the process. Aunt Elvera had cancer and no longer wanted treatment; she wanted to go the "natural" route to Jesus, not hooked up to machines that would artificially and temporarily keep her alive. Lisa and I were grateful that our parents had also chose to go "naturally"—and we were honored to be with them on their journey Home.

February 25

"For his anger is but for a moment, and his favor is for a lifetime. Weeping may tarry for the night, but joy comes with the morning."
Psalm 30:5

I often took Mom to a home-style restaurant for lunch. The food was great but she mostly loved their store where they had bins of polished rocks for sale. She loved rocks even more than books and sugar so after rushing through her meal she would hobble over to the bin. After sorting through the colorful rocks and putting them in a little velvet bag, you'd think she had a bag full of diamonds. In truth she would rather have the rocks. Darkness and light, always. While some days might feel overwhelmingly sad, just wait. Pure joy and God's blessings are always right around the corner.

February 26

"Even youths grow tired and weary, and young men stumble and fall; but those who hope in the Lord will renew their strength. They will soar on wings like eagles; they will run and not grow weary, they will walk and not be faint." **Isaiah 40:30** (NIV)

My son, Jason, called to tell me about a difficult visit he had with Dad in Memory Care. "Grandpa wanted me to take him home to see his mom. He said his car was out front and needed me to drive. But he also asked me about Grandma, so I wasn't sure who he meant." Jason said he was able to calm him down before he left by telling him a nurse would take him home. My son was upset; he and his grandpa had been close, regardless of distance. All I could do was pray for both of their losses that day.

February 27

"For you are my rock and my fortress; and for your name's sake you lead me and guide me; you take me out of the net they have hidden for me, for you are my refuge. Into your hand I commit my spirit; you have redeemed me, O Lord, faithful God." **Psalm 31:3-5**

After eating breakfast, Mom looked up from her newspaper and asked, "Aren't you my sister?" At first I thought she was joking because she usually knew who I was. Her sister was also at least 30 years older than me, not to mention, dead. But she wasn't joking. I asked, "Do you really think I'm Ruth Ann?" Mom looked at me a moment and laughed. "I guess I'm your mama, and I'm Lisa's mama, too, right?" I nodded and gave a little chuckle, while praying that my face wasn't showing how I really felt inside.

February 28

"The Lord is good, a stronghold in the day of trouble; he knows those who take refuge in him." **Nahum 1:7**

Things didn't seem right during my visit with Dad at Memory Care. His room wasn't clean but worse, Dad's feet and legs were very swollen from endless walking, searching. Each time I visited he seemed to be more and more gone, and I felt terrible leaving him alone. It was a cruel existence all around, but I was grateful that God "cushioned" my father's mind so he wouldn't know. Life is hard; the storms are inevitable, and the only way we can get through them is with Jesus Christ guiding us.

February 29

'As Jesus passed on from there, he saw a man called Matthew sitting at the tax booth, and he said to him, "Follow me." And he rose and followed him. " **Matthew 9:9**

When Mom moved into my apartment I knew I had to readjust my style. Everything was white and silver, from mirrored accessories to a giant white fur rug that she refused to walk on for fear of getting it dirty. I put most of it in storage, rug included and replaced my fancy chair with Mom's favorite brown recliner. I'd already left everything else in my previous California life behind, but now I was finally learning what it really meant to follow Jesus instead of 'me'. As a result, despite the difficulties to come I was happier and more at peace than I'd ever been in my life.

March

"Flowers appear on the earth; the season of singing has come, the cooing of doves is heard in our land." **Song of Songs 2: 12**

March 1

"Pray without ceasing," **1 Thessalonians 5:17**

I came by to check on Dad and was surprised to find him asleep in bed. He was lying on his back snoring and his shoes were still on. I didn't wake him but looking around his room I noticed there were three walkers: his old broken one, his new one, and another I'd never seen before. All but one of the pictures that were previously on the wall were scattered on the floor. It was March 2020 and things were about to get very bad not only for my father but also the world. Everyone needed prayer more than we could ever imagine.

March 2

"You blind Pharisee! First clean the inside of the cup and the plate, that the outside also may be clean." **Matthew 23:26**

It took me awhile to understand why I was so much happier in Texas. In California, life was glamorous, exciting, dynamic. I had lots of friends, but I never understood why I felt so empty and alone. Something was missing. Once I moved to Texas and began caregiving, everything in life changed for the better, including me. I was finally doing what Jesus told the Pharisee to do, working to improve my inside instead of the outside. Thank you, Jesus, for guiding me home!

March 3

"Likewise the Spirit helps us in our weakness. For we do not know what to pray for as we ought, but the Spirit himself intercedes for us with groanings too deep for words." **Romans 8:26**

Things were intense between spending time with Dad and leaving Mom alone too long. I was very worried about my dad; he'd only been in Memory Care a few weeks but there were already signs he was being neglected. His room was filthy; some of his personal items were broken, including a lamp. And if I ever found staff at all they were usually watching television and acted upset that I'd bothered them. Moving him wasn't an options; he was considered a 'trouble case' and nothing else was available. I spent more time praying than sleeping; my family needed my help and I needed help from God.

March 4

"You have put more joy in my heart than they have when their grain and wine abound." **Psalm 4:7**

I took Mom to a wonderful store in Jefferson called 'Made in the Shade' where they have a giant outdoor 'mining sluice' and you can purchase a bag of dirt mixed with gemstones. I watched as Mom lowered her first tray of dirt into the water, sloshing it around to uncover an enormous chunk of quartz, along with polished rocks and even a few fossils. Seeing her newly revealed treasures, she slumped over and started crying. I ran over to hold her up but she was happy, overcome by what she'd found. Over the next year we went back several times until she couldn't make the car trip anymore. But oh, what a joy seeing my mother so unabashedly happy over such simple things.

March 5

"She looks well to the ways of her household and does not eat the bread of idleness." **Proverbs 31:27**

One of my strangest ways of de-stressing is to clean house: dusting, sweeping and mopping. This was difficult when Mom first moved in with me because she wanted to help but was still recovering from a back injury. The way I solved it was by setting up a new jigsaw puzzle and have her search for all of the end pieces. Unfortunately by the time I finished cleaning her back hurt from being hunched over the table searching for puzzle pieces. I prayed for God to ease my guilt as I placed a pain patch on her back--but least she was in pain in a clean house.

March 6

"So, whether you eat or drink, or whatever you do, do all to the glory of God." **1 Corinthians 10:31**

My son is an excellent cook, partly because I was such a bad one. He grew up instinctively knowing which seasonings were missing from his bowl of SpaghettiOs or plate of Hamburger Helper. Frankly I'm not sure how I kept the boy alive. I felt the same about Mom, having to come up with 3 healthy meals a day when I usually only ate once. With constant prayer for guidance, I changed my lifestyle in every direction. I became a much better cook and caregiver, and today even my son likes my cooking. Praise God for His wonderful life-changing miracles.

March 7

"He himself bore our sins in his body on the tree, that we might die to sin and live to righteousness. By his wounds you have been healed." **1 Peter 2:24**

Nurse Lindsey asked me to call one of her patients whose husband was being admitted into the psychiatric hospital. She sounded frightened when I called, not knowing what to expect. I explained the basics, including what to bring, visiting hours and rules. Then I asked about her relationship with Jesus. She said she believed so I told her, "That alone is half the battle. Your husband can go through the process, do what the doctors tell him to do, detox, try his best. But without Jesus helping both of you, it will all fall apart soon after." We prayed. I'm not sure what happened to them, but if they allowed God to lead, I have faith they are both well today.

March 8

"Show yourself in all respects to be a model of good works, and in your teaching show integrity, dignity, and sound speech that cannot be condemned, so that an opponent may be put to shame, having nothing evil to say about us." **Titus 2:7-8**

One of Mom's former students, Chris Barton, sent me a sweet message about attending our former high school's One Act Play competition. He said he was thinking of 'Mrs. Brown' and how much she would have loved being there. He was right. In addition to English and Spanish, Mom also taught Theater Arts and directed award-winning plays. I still get messages from students like Chris all over the U.S. telling me how impactful she was on their lives, that she made them strive to be better people. I'm forever blessed to be remembered as "Mrs. Brown's daughter".

March 9

"For I consider that the sufferings of this present time are not worth comparing with the glory that is to be revealed to us." **Romans 8:18**

A friend in California died from complications of Multiple Sclerosis. We were both diagnosed with MS around the same time and our symptoms were similar, but in recent years she took a swift downturn. At the time, Mom was beginning a toddler-like phase of Alzheimer's. I wasn't able to grieve or cry in front of her about losing my friend; she'd never understand. So just as I would learn to do when I later lost several other friends, I had to tamp down the pain, find pockets of time to mourn, and pictured my friend in Heaven without her wheelchair, standing, dancing, whole again. No more pain or suffering, just praising Jesus face-to-face. Hallelujah.

March 10

"I know that the Lord will maintain the cause of the afflicted and will execute justice for the needy." **Psalm 140:12**

The last few times I visited Dad he was sleeping. A nurse said he stayed up all night walking, searching for whoever it was he had lost. In my heart I knew it was Mom, but I had to remind myself that even when they were still together he left their room looking for "someone". I felt tremendous guilt, always trying to figure out if there was a better way for him, a better place, so he wasn't all alone. If Mom could have lived with Lisa, I would have stayed with Dad 24/7. I would never have left his side to make sure he ate, was able to use the toilet, and stayed clean. But all I could do was pray for God to ease my guilt and frustrations, and to protect my poor father…

March 11

"Be still and know that I am God. I will be exalted among the nations, I will be exalted in the earth!" **Psalm 46:10**

Lisa kept Mom a few days so I could try to rest but I was so consumed with worry that all I did at night was pace, agitated. Everything in my bedroom was spotless; nothing left to clean or organize. The sun was up, another night had come and gone without sleep. I sat on the bed and opened my bible to Psalm 46:10: *Be still and know that I am God.* I knew I needed to stop, to give myself a break and let God take over. I drove to Hobby Lobby and bought the largest block letters they had. I came home and hammered two words over my bed: BE STILL. And that was that. It was 3pm but I crawled in bed, still in my clothes, and for the first time in months I fell into a deep, peaceful sleep.

March 12

"Then they cried to the Lord in their trouble, and he delivered them from their distress. He brought them out of darkness and the shadow of death and burst their bonds apart." **Psalm 107:13-14**

I had only missed two days of visiting Dad but when I returned everything was wrong. His false teeth were missing; there were several cold trays of food but without teeth he couldn't eat. His room was even more filthy that before. I ran out of the room looking for help and found someone who said he'd take care of everything, but later learned no one ever did. Not long after, the pandemic shut down the world and in doing so, locked my dad away from protection. The way I handled it was by locking it out of my head. Maybe God was cushioning me from things I had no control over but this was by far the hardest part of caregiving for me. I prayed, and for now had to let it go.

March 13

"Jesus said to them, "My food is to do the will of him who sent me and to accomplish his work." **John 4:34**

My friends knew I was stressed so they tried to plan a trip to the lake for my upcoming birthday. Mom overheard me talking about it and was afraid I was going to leave her alone. Even after napping, she woke up and asked, "Are you going to make me go away when you go to the lake?" One night she was spiraling so much I had to stop and pray about it and then realized she was hungry. I cooked her favorite pork chops and cinnamon apples and that did it; she was happy again. After that, I kept cookies on hand for emergencies, praising God for such simple solutions to complex problems.

March 14

"The night is far gone; the day is at hand. So then let us cast off the works of darkness and put on the armor of light." **Romans 13:12**

It was 2020 and the world was slowly starting to shut down. I took Mom to lunch at her favorite Luby's cafeteria, a place that sadly wouldn't survive the pandemic. For the first time, we didn't have to wait in line because there were only 4 of us in the entire place. Mom didn't understand why some of the workers were wearing surgeon masks; it was already starting to scare her. That day I refused to allow fear to penetrate what was left of her life. After lunch we went to the grocery store where she got to drive an electric cart, laughing and happy. We never know what will happen tomorrow, but with God's help I would try to make every day as beautiful as possible for Mom and me, pandemic or not.

March 15

"And I tell you, you are Peter, and on this rock I will build my church, and the gates of hell shall not prevail against it." **Matthew 16:18**

During the early days of the pandemic I was surprised to learn that most of our local churches were already closed. I understood wanting to be 'safe' but our community churches were the one place people needed in time of crisis and fear. It seemed there could have been better ways for people to worship other than watching online, even if it meant sitting in cars in a church parking lot with a pastor using a megaphone to preach. What happened to Matthew writing about how *the gates of hell shall not prevail* against the church? Back then I prayed that this would never happen again, and my prayer remains the same today.

March 16

"Return to your stronghold, O prisoners of hope; today I declare that I will restore to you double." **Zechariah 9:12**

It had been days since my last visit with Dad. After finding him so neglected I allowed fear and trauma to keep me away. I also felt like a plate-spinner from the Ed Sullivan show, trying to keep those plates in the air. I had to keep Mom happy and balanced, fed and clean while trying to keep myself healthy enough to handle everything. But then I'd picture Dad, left all alone, and all the plates would fall down. Now, I realize I had a version of PTSD after seeing him in such bad shape; I coped by pretending everything was okay, while praying until I fell sleep at night for God to take better care of my dad than I could…

March 17

"Now faith is the assurance of things hoped for, the conviction of things not seen. For by it the people of old received their commendation. By faith we understand that the universe was created by the word of God, so that what is seen was not made out of things that are visible." **Hebrews 11:1-3**

Memory Care was now on lockdown so I wasn't able to visit Dad at all. I was already traumatized about what happened when I only missed a few days, and now no one would be able to follow-up at all. Before lockdown I talked to one of his nurses who only said, "Mr. Brown's just being Mr. Brown, wandering around." I was too afraid to ask if he had eaten, or if his room was clean. I prayed on my knees for my father because now, more than ever, he was in The Father's hands.

March 18

"For the word of the cross is folly to those who are perishing, but to us who are being saved it is the power of God." **1 Corinthians 1:18**

In the early days of the pandemic things were as normal as possible, in a completely un-normal way. Mom was happily working on her jigsaw puzzles but she was also having trouble distinguishing between night and day. Lisa had an ear infection and back then if you had a slight fever for any reason everyone panicked, so she didn't want to visit. Some stores were still open so I bought as many supplies as possible and the rest were delivered. Mostly, I prayed that God would keep the "normal" in our little world as steady as possible, because the rest of our outside world was about to go insane.

March 19

"I sought the Lord, and he answered me and delivered me from all my fears." **Psalm 34:4**

Fear is like the monster under your bed when you're a child. There's nothing there, it's your imagination that keeps you awake. For many, myself included, March 2020 was very much like that monster. Texas was now on full lock-down. Grocery stores were running out of basic supplies and people were afraid to leave their homes, not even to just step outside and breathe the air. For me, all my fears were focused on my father, alone in an already neglectful Memory Care facility. I found solace reading the book of Psalm and listening to my mother singing gospel songs in the room next to mine. God repeatedly told us to "have no fear" so I did my best to obey.

March 20

"Listen to advice and accept instruction, that you may gain wisdom in the future." **Proverbs 19:20**

In the midst of everything, I received a group text from a friend asking for prayers for boyfriend problems. Other than this, I hadn't heard from her at all. I vented about this on the phone to my friend Paula. "You need to pray for her," she said. "Friends are like M&M's; they're not all alike. They aren't all meant to be your best friends. Maybe she's just a regular friend who you can't count on for anything real, so don't expect it. That doesn't mean she's a bad friend, but it sounds like you might have to be a better one to her." What a great lesson. Ironically, I completely forgot to ask Paula how she was doing first. Thank you, Lord, for always sending us Wise Counsel when we need it.

March 21

"And Jesus said to him, "If you can'! All things are possible for one who believes." **Mark 9:23**

Soon after moving to Texas I held an event for my birthday that I will forever call the 'Celebrate Every Day' party. It started with a tiny budget but after turning everything over to Jesus, it quickly evolved into something almost miraculous. Without even trying, what was originally meant to be a small gathering turned into a mega-event with 50+ friends and family, a free venue in a hotel, free desserts, free drinks, and enough food to feed homeless people after. New friendships were made that day, including meeting my dear Tina Bryan. I believe God knew I was going to need something extra special from Him to help get me through the next few years, even if it was 'only' an incredible, unforgettable celebration.

March 22

"But you, O Lord, do not be far off! O you my help, come quickly to my aid!" **Psalm 22:19**

Mom fell again. This time she was working on a puzzle when I saw her slowly falling backward in her chair. There was nothing I could do but watch as she bumped into another chair on her way down, landing on her back. There were no serious injuries, nothing broken, but Mom was panicking, demanding that I call an ambulance. I had to remind her that because of the pandemic we didn't "live in that world" anymore. I couldn't get her up so I called Nurse Lindsey. She came over and expertly got Mom back on her feet, soon laughing and joking and absolutely fine. I thanked God that Lindsey wasn't afraid to come help us; many others were. These were strange times, but with His help we would all survive.

March 23

"I have said these things to you, that in me you may have peace. In the world you will have tribulation. But take heart; I have overcome the world." **John 16:33**

The day after Mom fell, hospice called to tell me that Dad had fallen again in Memory Care. The nurse said he wasn't hurt but he rarely slept in his room anymore. She said he wandered most of the night and was usually found slumped over in the chair seat of his walker or on a couch in the lobby. I was certain that the reason he didn't sleep in his room was because he couldn't find it anymore. I asked if they'd found his bottom teeth; she didn't know so I told her to make sure someone was helping him eat. She assured me she would. All I could do was trust everyone involved, and I prayed continually that the nursing staff would show my father the kindness and respect he deserved.

March 24

"Though he fall, he shall not be cast headlong, for the Lord upholds his hand. **Psalm 37:24**

Mom was still sore and shaky from her fall, but mostly she was afraid of falling again. I spent large portions of the day trying to keep her fears at bay. At the same time Lisa was afraid that her son, Zack, might lose his job due to the pandemic. What I tried to convey to both of them was not to allow all the "what ifs" in life to frighten us. Without peace from Christ, none of us would survive anything, pandemic or not. I said prayers of gratitude because after turning everything over to Him, I wasn't afraid anymore.

March 25

"Behold, I am sending you out as sheep in the midst of wolves, so be wise as serpents and innocent as doves." **Matthew 10:16**

Memory Care had been locked down a little over one week and Dad had already fallen 5 times. I was told he had a cut on his face and was losing too much weight. After continual urging, hospice finally put in an order for someone to feed him while I prayed they would find his teeth so he could chew. They were also increasing his medication and hospice visits to 5 times a week, assuring me they would take good care of him. There was nothing I could do other than trust in God, because I sadly didn't trust any of them anymore.

March 26

"So we do not lose heart. Though our outer self is wasting away, our inner self is being renewed day by day." 2 **Corinthians 4:16**

Hospice called and said Dad was dying so they snuck Lisa and me into Memory Care to say goodbye. My worst fears were confirmed when we found his room even worse than before, and it was terrible then. But much worse, Dad was skeletal, bruised, cuts everywhere. In only 9 days of lock-down he looked completely different. If anyone had actually been taking care of him they would have known how bad things were. But no one did anything other than call to tell me about his falls. He didn't die that night; he sat up babbling, crazed, while Lisa and I tried to calm him. The only grace was that we got to pray for him and said goodbye before he drifted back to sleep. We prayed together, asking God to help us forgive ourselves for things so very far out of our control…

March 27

"Love bears all things, believes all things, hopes all things, endures all things." **1 Corinthians 13:7**

It was very early, around 2 a.m. when I came home from Memory Care. I was surprised to find Mom still up, waiting for me. She was afraid and wanted to know where I'd been. I did my best to explain what was happening but she was mostly confused and didn't understand who was dying. The last year with Dad had been more difficult for her than any of us would ever know; it seemed she had blocked out most of her memories of their marriage to help her heal. But as I was leaving her room she said, "We were married 53 years, how could I forget that?" I held her tight and we cried together, feeling a mixture of gratitude and sadness for her that she finally remembered...

March 28

"He will wipe away every tear from their eyes, and death shall be no more, neither shall there be mourning, nor crying, nor pain anymore, for the former things have passed away." **Revelation21:4**

And then, my father died, very peacefully. No more pain, no more searching or suffering. Again, Lisa and I were allowed to be there; his room had been completely scrubbed clean but we could still smell things under the bleach and ammonia. No matter how neglectfully he'd been treated in that place, I have to believe that between Alzheimer's, medication, and the prayers surrounding him, he didn't know the difference anymore. He didn't know whether he was clean or dirty, and I pray he didn't feel abandoned or alone in the end. For now, I focused my prayers on healing for Lisa, Mom and me, that He would relieve our hearts and minds of those last painful memories.

March 29

"Love one another with brotherly affection. Outdo one another in showing honor." **Romans 12:10**

Our friends rallied and helped like never before, bringing food and offering help with funeral arrangements. Jason and Mimi brought us groceries, including now-rare pandemic items like paper towels. Mom was napping much, waking up asking things like, "Are you keeping that cloth on your head?" and naming her dead family members: "Mama, Daddy, my brother..." She repeatedly asked me if her father was still alive and instead of compassionately lying, I was like the Angel of Death telling her over and over that he died in the mid-1970's. Those were death-filled days and I was grateful for the peace that only Christ, family, and friends could bring

March 30

"The Lord will fight for you, and you have only to be silent." **Exodus 14:14**

Jason and Mimi brought us a delicious pork roast dinner for Lisa's birthday. Mom ate most of hers and then for the first time since moving in with me she wanted to go to bed without watching television or eating a bowl of Blue Bell. Lisa and I helped her to bed and, again surprisingly, she asked me to turn off her reading light. Our hearts were breaking for her. She was grieving but she didn't even know why, or for whom. After everyone left I spent the rest of the night in prayer, thanking and praising God for giving me this new life as my mother's caregiver. With His help, I would make sure she would find joy and happiness again.

March 31

"Even though I walk through the valley of the shadow of death, I will fear no evil, for you are with me; your rod and your staff, they comfort me."
Psalm 23:4

I hadn't slept all night. While preparing for Dad's funeral and in a very cruel twist, I lost a friendship in California. I was grieving and exhausted. Then at 5am Mom knocked on my door asking, "Are you getting ready to go to town to see Daddy?" I couldn't think of anything to say other than, "No Mom, not this morning," and put her back to bed. She looked so tiny and frail. I got on my knees and prayed for help; I couldn't do this alone. I was grieving my dad, the loss of a friend, and preparing to care for my mother on my own. This was hard, but I knew the only way I'd regain my strength was by holding tight to Jesus' hand. While praying I already felt stronger. I would survive.

April

"A Psalm for giving thanks. Make a joyful noise to the Lord, all the earth! Serve the Lord with gladness! Come into his presence with singing!" **Psalm 100: 1-2**

April 1

"Then David and the people who were with him raised their voices and wept until they had no more strength to weep." 1 **Samuel 30:4**

It was the day before Dad's funeral and Mom woke up sad again without understanding why. I took her out for Andy's custard which made her happy, but on the drive back she said she was worried about having to go "back out in the woods" to live with her mama. It was heartbreaking; giant chunks of her life were leaving, possibly faster from stress and grief. Once home I asked Lisa to come over and help; I needed some time alone. I broke down after listening to the Prince song, 'Sometimes It Snows in April', which will forever remind me of Dad. And that night I cried and prayed until I felt His grace take over and finally, I slept. Peacefully.

April 2

"So also you have sorrow now, but I will see you again, and your hearts will rejoice, and no one will take your joy from you." **John 16:22**

Dad's pandemic graveside-only funeral was exactly what our Navy Chief Petty Officer father would have wanted, beginning with an Honor Guard and a 3-gun salute. Mom cried and seemed to understand what was happening, but the 45-minute drive home was rough. Like a toddler, she was angry about being in the car for so long and wanted to know why we were 'so far out in the woods'. I prayed for patience, and then realized she was probably hungry. We had a refrigerator packed with food at home but I stopped at Sonic and got her a cheeseburger and milkshake. She was fine, happily eating in the car. I thanked God for the toddler years with my son; I would need so much of that information in my final years with my mother.

April 3

"He is the radiance of the glory of God and the exact imprint of his nature, and he upholds the universe by the word of his power. After making purification for sins, he sat down at the right hand of the Majesty on high,"
Hebrews 1:3

It was now two years after Dad died and so much had changed. I bought a house and Lisa moved in with Mom and me. And after a bout with Covid, Mom contracted a cough that never went away. But that spring (and every spring to follow) we planted a gardens with tomatoes, peppers and lots of flowers. Finally, Mom began to bloom, too. She was happy for the first time in years and Lisa and I were happy again, too. Those storms were rough and some days it was difficult to remember what the light looked like--but now, the light was almost blinding. Praise God!

April 4

"And he said to them, "Do not be alarmed. You seek Jesus of Nazareth, who was crucified. He has risen; he is not here. See the place where they laid him." **Mark 16:6**

The three of us went to a beautiful Easter church service followed by lunch at a local Mexican restaurant. Mom found a quarter in the parking lot which made her giddy, happily showing the quarter to people on the way inside. At home, we had an Easter egg hunt for Mom. After, she sat on the patio opening her colorful plastic eggs, excited about finding the little trinkets inside. She had no memory that they were all things we found in her jewelry box. It was a beautiful Easter with reminders that everything old is new again. Thank you, Jesus, for living, dying, and rising again for all of us. Amen.

April 5

"Let us know; let us press on to know the Lord; his going out is sure as the dawn; he will come to us as the showers, as the spring rains that water the earth." **Hosea 6:3**

Mom and I went shopping for gardening supplies and after we went to her beloved bookstore where she bought several books. On the way home we drove through her other favorite place in town, Andy's Custard, a trip we would make dozens of times over the years. Happily eating her vanilla custard, Mom said, "It was a fun day. I've lived a really good life overall!" This was the most positive thing she'd said in a long time and I thanked God for those lovely simple things in life that make such a difference.

April 6

"He has told you, O man, what is good; and what does the Lord require of you but to do justice, and to love kindness, and to walk humbly with your God?" **Micah 6:8**

I was having a bad day with MS so I worked on a patio project to distract me from the pain. Mom came out to 'help' but I didn't want her to get hurt. I brought out the book she was reading and had her sit near me. But after asking several more times if she could help I was short with her. "Do you think it's time for me to go to a nursing home?" she asked, tears in her eyes. I stopped what I was doing. I couldn't allow anything, not even my own pain, to hurt my mother. I prayed for Jesus to give me the words to fix it and chose honesty. "Mom, I'm having a rough day. Would you go on a walk with me?" Suddenly, she was my mother again. She hugged me and we took a happy little walk together.

April 7

"A soft answer turns away wrath, but a harsh word stirs up anger."
Proverbs 15:1

Mom loved Dollar Tree because she could buy lots of books there. I was on another aisle and heard her ask a worker to get a book off the top shelf for her. The worker angrily said, "What, do you expect me to lift you up, lady?" I ran around the corner to see the woman hand Mom 3 books before going back to stocking shelves. Thankfully, Mom was oblivious and went to another aisle. I prayed hard before approaching the worker and said, "You were mean to my mother." She started to defend herself but I added, "We all have our burdens; I'm sure you do, too. But that lady you were so rude to has Alzheimer's and a little kindness goes a long way." She just shrugged and kept working. I prayed, grateful that Jesus kept me from kicking her…

April 8

"Therefore take up the whole armor of God, that you may be able to withstand in the evil day, and having done all, to stand firm."
Ephesians 6:13

It was time to sign Mom up for hospice. The dry, hacking cough she contracted after Covid led to advanced COPD. Even though she quit smoking 30+ years earlier, her doctor said lung disease was probably dormant until Covid brought it out. I instantly thought of Dad and how hospice had neglected him, but this time Lisa and I would be there to monitor Mom's care. She would never be alone, and although Lisa worked fulltime I would be home 24/7 to administer all her medications. God had prepared Lisa and me tremendously for what was to come. We had no fear. We were ready.

April 9

"When you pass through the waters, I will be with you; and through the rivers, they shall not overwhelm you; when you walk through fire you shall not be burned, and the flame shall not consume you." **Isaiah 43:2**

I was scrubbing cabinets when I heard Mom having a terrible coughing fit in her room. I found her shaking, struggling to breathe. I helped her to the living room and gave her a breathing treatment then put her on oxygen, the way hospice showed me the day before. When finished she was exhausted so I covered her with a blanket and sat next to her, holding her hand and praying as she fell asleep. This, I would soon learn, was to be our daily routine to the end. It reminded me of the ocean tide, coming in and going out, unstoppable. But with God's help, I would learn to ride the waves and trust in Him to keep us all from drowning.

April 10

"And this is the confidence that we have toward him, that if we ask anything according to his will he hears us. And if we know that he hears us in whatever we ask, we know that we have the requests that we have asked of him."
1 John 5:14-15

I kept a baby monitor by my bed connected to Mom's room. Early one morning I heard her praying; she was thanking Jesus for her blessings but was also asking Him to help her. I went in immediately and, still praying, Mom said, "Thank you, Jesus, for sending the help I asked for!" I laid on her bed with her until she finished praying. For now she was finally calm, no coughing, no uncontrollable shaking. Thank you Jesus, Amen.

April 11

"Ask, and it will be given to you; seek, and you will find; knock, and it will be opened to you. For everyone who asks receives, and the one who seeks finds, and to the one who knocks it will be opened." **Matthew 7:7-8**

We now had two wonderful hospice nurses, Heather and Leslie, who would become invaluable blessings for us. Each visit Mom would talk to them about her teaching years and the only students she remembered, the 'three bad boys'. Laughing, she claimed she hit one of them with a stick. She also turned her best teacher friend, Mrs. Griffis, into someone named "Doreen Sharp", a name Lisa and I never heard before. Mom's nurses were patient and kind and loved visiting with our still-funny mother. God was supplying us with everyone and everything we would need for the difficult road ahead of us.

April 12

"But they who wait for the Lord shall renew their strength; they shall mount up with wings like eagles; they shall run and not be weary; they shall walk and not faint."
Isaiah 40:31

Mom coughed through her breakfast and had a very difficult time breathing the rest of the day. Nighttime was even worse because she was getting up every few minutes to turn off her oxygen machine (after playing with the dials). She was shaky and restless, while at the same time so very tired. This went on all night and into the early morning when she finally fell asleep, exhausted. I prayed for clarity, help, and soon learned that her restlessness was due to the steroid breathing treatments I was giving her before bed, something I immediately changed. Those early learning days and nights were exhausting for both of us.

April 13

"Trust in him at all times, O people; pour out your heart before him; God is a refuge for us. Selah" **Psalm 62:8**

Throughout the spring major storms passed through our area, knocking out power and damaging farms and houses, including our roof which had to be replaced due to hail damage. But then, sunshine. One morning Mom got up early singing her new favorite song, "Cool, Clear Water". No coughing, no breathing treatment, and only a brief time on oxygen after we took a little walk down the road. The storms are part of life, in the world and in our lives. And then, sunshine. Selah.

April 14

"Grandchildren are the crown of the aged, and the glory of children is their fathers." **Proverbs 17:6**

I was overcome with joy after seeing the first ultrasounds of my new grandson. When Jason was in high school I was already looking forward to being a grandmother someday. I even fixed up a little room under the staircase of my California house, painting fun murals on the walls and picturing my grandchild playing in there someday. But now, it was actually happening. Admittedly I wasn't the greatest mother; I was too busy following my path instead of God's. But now, I was new. Now, I was ready to be the grandmother, and mother, and daughter, that God always expected of me. I may have blown other areas of my life, but as a follower of Jesus Christ, I am forever redeemed.

April 15

"But if it is by grace, it is no longer on the basis of works; otherwise grace would no longer be grace." **Romans 11:6**

Hospice delivered a hospital bed to the house for Mom and I was very concerned. It was used and looked that way. The mattress had some type of uncleanable stain and the frame was dented and scratched. But I did my best to make it pretty with new sheets, a matching floral comforter, and a strand of purple silk flowers around the frame. When it was ready, Lisa brought Mom in and she immediately started crying. I thought she hated it, but it was the opposite. "Why do I get something so special?" she asked. She took off her shoes and carefully lay down on her "new" bed, saying how nice and comfortable it was. Oh, what grace!

April 16

"And these words that I command you today shall be on your heart. You shall teach them diligently to your children, and shall talk of them when you sit in your house, and when you walk by the way, and when you lie down, and when you rise." **Deuteronomy 6:6-7**

I watched the Thornton Wilder play, 'Our Town' and one part grabbed me by the heart. The ghost of the main character 'Emily' goes back in time to when she was young and living with her family. She noticed that no one was paying attention to each other and urged them to talk, not to take for granted the short amount of time they had together. But they couldn't hear or see her, and eventually she had to leave, realizing we usually don't understand our mortality until it's too late. Life on earth is short. We must "see" and "hear" each other now--or wait to be together in Heaven.

April 17

"Oh, taste and see that the Lord is good! Blessed is the man who takes refuge in him." **Psalm 34:8**

Mom was doing really well breathing-wise so I took her on one of her favorite outings, an estate sale. She found a few books and a dish to hold some of her beloved rocks, and then told me she wanted a hamburger. We went to a drive-thru and by then it was pouring rain. At home, she kept saying her burger was delicious and how happy she was, praising God for such a fun day. Jesus taught me so many important lessons like this in my caregiving years, especially the importance of appreciating the smaller, easier days--rain or shine.

April 18

"Whoever gives thought to the word will discover good, and blessed is he who trusts in the Lord." **Proverbs 16:20**

After a bad night of coughing and breathing attacks, Nurse Heather came to check on Mom. She said her left lung was getting bad so from then on I began giving her 3 breathing treatments a day and kept her on oxygen almost 24/7. In spite of that, Mom's spirits remained very good. Every day we worked on collage jigsaw puzzles, and although she couldn't go on long walks anymore she was still able to wander around the backyard a little. God blessed us in so many beautiful ways, with flowers and music and laughter. Through everything, He was always there.

April 19

"For who is God, but the Lord? And who is a rock, except our God?"
Psalm 18:31

Mom needed new clothes so we went shopping. She rode an electric scooter in the store and had so much fun, and even when she almost ran over several people they laughed and talked to her. But that night around 3 a.m. she was coughing badly. After several breathing treatments and oxygen she fell asleep, but I stayed up reading about the end stages of COPD. If she only had Alzheimer's she could live many more years, but with a combination of COPD (and Congestive Heart Failure) it was going to get rough. I prayed that Lisa and I would be prepared, and I prayed for peace, asking Jesus to lift me above all fears. Almost immediately, I slept until the sun came up. Thank you, Jesus, amen.

April 20

"Follow God's example, therefore, as dearly loved children."
Ephesians 5:1

Out of nowhere, Mom started talking about getting a puppy. No idea why. I told her I'd be happy to get her a puppy if she agreed to take it outside 2-3 times a day and clean up after it. She paused and said she actually wanted a fake puppy, not a real one. I found a stuffed dog she bought a few months earlier and brought it to her. She hugged it tight and carried it with her the rest of the day, just like a little girl. My mother had never been ultra-maternal; she was strong, feisty and independent. My prayer that night was that God would continually adjust my heart and mind to every phase Mom would be going through, just as she did for me.

April 21

"For just as we share abundantly in the sufferings of Christ, so also our comfort abounds through Christ."
2 Corinthians 1:5

Early morning Mom was coughing horribly. This time it sounded watery, like bronchitis. I gave her every treatment and medication available but she was still struggling and suffering. Finally I called hospice and while I was on the phone I heard her from the baby monitor praying, "This hurts so much, please help me Jesus." Before running to help her I got on my knees and prayed the exact same prayer...

April 22

"He has saved us and called us to a holy life—not because of anything we have done but because of his own purpose and grace. This grace was given us in Christ Jesus before the beginning of time." **2 Timothy 1:9**

Mom and I both slept through the night, halleluiah! Not only that, but she also told me she was feeling so good she wanted "some of that good ice cream". I took her to Andy's, and the joy on her face as she ate her vanilla custard made up for every moment of pain and sorrow from the night before. And such is life, from darkness to light. Praise God.

April 23

"Children's children are a crown to the aged,
and parents are the pride of their children."
Proverbs 17:6

I dreamed about my paternal grandmother "MeeMaw" again. This time Jason was with me as a little boy. We both hugged MeeMaw and it seemed I could even smell her perfume. I asked her what made her always smelled so pretty and, smiling but with tears in her eyes, she said she loved taking 'her baths' but she could only take showers now. It was comforting getting a little 'visit' from her; I needed it. One of my continual prayers is that I will be as loved and respected by my grandchildren as my MeeMaw was to hers.

April 24

"So then, banish anxiety from your heart and cast off the troubles of your body, for youth and vigor are meaningless." **Ecclesiastes 11:10**

It was a horrible night with Mom. She coughed endlessly but this time she also had a fever. Nurse Heather was scheduled for the next morning so I decided to wait for her, but something was definitely wrong. Neither of us slept. I spent the night and early morning by her bed giving her breathing treatments and watching YouTube videos about COPD again. What I learned was that the ultimate battle would be staving off pneumonia. I also learned that I needed to stop watching videos about COPD. I refocused and prayed that Mom didn't have pneumonia.

April 25

Blessed are those whose way is blameless, who walk in the law of the Lord! Blessed are those who keep his testimonies, who seek him with their whole heart, who also do no wrong, but walk in his ways! **Psalm 119:1-3**

Mom didn't have pneumonia this time but she did have bronchitis and began a new round of antibiotics. As always, nurses Heather and Leslie were on call for us day or night. They were (and are) nurses with true hearts for the elderly, something vital in their work. Our family had experienced the opposite with Dad, with a nursing staff that didn't care. I thank God for all nurses who take the word "caregiving" literally, like the wonderful nurses who cared for my mother.

April 26

"The Lord will always lead you; He will satisfy your needs in dry lands and give strength to your bones. You will be like a garden that has much water, like a spring that never runs dry." **Isaiah 57: 11 (NCV)**

I was having a very rare lunch with a friend. When the check came, I was searching in my purse for a credit card and found $50 cash in the side pocket. I had no idea where it came from and even asked my friend if she put it there. She didn't know what I was talking about so I stuck it in my wallet. Later in the grocery card I started to pay and found another $40 in that same once-empty side pocket of my purse! To this day I don't have any idea where all that money came from, but perhaps God was showing me that He wouldn't allow me to run out of anything I'd need to survive what was coming--beginning with a purse full of money...

April 27

"And if we know that he hears us—whatever we ask—we know that we have what we asked of him." **1 John 5:15**

It started out a wonderful day after taking Mom to the beauty shop for a haircut. When we got home I gave her a breathing treatment and all was well. But after dinner she began acting strange. She said she heard a loud roaring sound outside and got angry that we couldn't hear it. She insisted there was some type of "machine" outside so we all went out to check. Nothing was there which only made her madder. I thought she maybe got water in her ear at the beauty shop so I called hospice to check her in the morning. After helping her to bed, we prayed together that the roaring sound would subside and she was finally calm enough to fall asleep.

April 28

"In the morning, Lord, you hear my voice; in the morning I lay my requests before you and wait expectantly." **Psalm 5:3**

Hospice came over and checked Mom's ears. The good news was that there was no sign of infection. But as soon as Mom put her hearing aids back in she heard the roaring sound again--and that's when the lights came on for me. I placed Mom's hearing aids in my own ears and sure enough, I heard the same loud rushing sound she described--but it was because a battery was missing in one of them. After replacing both, no more rushing. I could certainly understand why she'd been so angry and frustrated; the roaring sound was definitely real and very loud. As soon as Mom put the hearing aids back in, she was happy again and wanted to go outside. We sat in our rocking chairs and she sang a bit. God is so very, very good. All the time.

April 29

"Every good gift and every perfect gift is from above, coming down from the Father of lights, with whom there is no variation or shadow due to change." **James 1:17**

Mom wasn't able to walk outside anymore so Heather ordered a wheelchair for her. This was one of the biggest blessings of the entire year for both of us. Mom was free, and I wasn't confined to the house anymore either. I took her on the first of what we'd call our "Walk and Rolls" around the block. She was so happy, the wind blowing her silver hair while she looked at nature. The chair was very easy to push, and it was good for me to get out walking again, too. Thank you, God, for always finding ways to make the hard parts so much easier.

April 30

"Through him then let us continually offer up a sacrifice of praise to God, that is, the fruit of lips that acknowledge his name." **Hebrews 13:15**

Each time I noticed Mom getting depresses I took her on a wheelchair walk before the rains hit. She never remembered our walks from one day to the next, even if I showed her pictures from the day before. So it was "brand new" every time and she was immediately joyful. As we rolled along, I talked to her about all of our blessings—our beautiful home, our family, and soon her first great-grandchild would be born. Smiling happily, she raised her hands up in the air and said, "Praise God, praise God!" Yes, praise God!

"If I then, your Lord and Teacher, have washed your feet, you also ought to wash one another's feet." **John 13:14**

May 1

"Above all, keep loving one another earnestly, since love covers a multitude of sins." **1 Peter 4:8**

Mom began talking about how Lisa and I grew up with her parents when we were babies. This wasn't true, and at first I tried correcting her, ignoring the rule to 'never argue with dementia'. I felt like it was somehow lying to go along with her incorrect memories. But then I thought of how I "lied" to her when I hid polished rocks outside, convincing her they were there naturally. She happily believed it. And I "lied" (by omission) about her disease, never letting her know she had Alzheimer's. So now, whenever Mom said something completely absurd about our lives, I prayed to find ways to answer with kindness and compassion for a disease that sadly defies common sense.

May 2

"For if you forgive other people when they sin against you, your heavenly Father will also forgive you."
Matthew 6:14

A nurse from Mom's former doctor's office called regarding an appointment. I never wanted to hear from that office again and told the nurse my reasons. After Mom had Covid he prescribed codeine cough syrup for her lingering cough. It never helped but he refused to send her to a pulmonary specialist, telling me she was "old with allergies". I explained to the nurse that after finally seeing a specialist, Mom was diagnosed with late-stage COPD and was now on hospice. She apologized and I could tell she was sincere. I prayed that Jesus could help me forgive all the healthcare workers who didn't care about either of my parents and praised Him for the ones who did.

May 3

"He put a new song in my mouth, a song of praise to our God. Many will see and fear, and put their trust in the Lord." **Psalm 40:3**

Still wearing her nightgown, Mom got in her wheelchair and began feeling around the arms, pushing on it. She asked me what happened to the on/off switch and said the 'beeper' was missing, too. Apparently she thought it was her electric scooter from Assisted Living. When she tried to wheel herself outside I reminded her she was still wearing her nightie. She looked down at herself and laughed. I helped her up, got her changed, and we went on a long Walk and Roll around the block. She had me pick up a stick so she could 'conduct' along the way as she sang her favorite gospel songs. What a blessing.

May 4

"And though a man might prevail against one who is alone, two will withstand him—a threefold cord is not quickly broken." **Ecclesiastes 4:12**

My friends often tried to get together with me but I always told them I couldn't. Beyond taking care of Mom, I felt like I didn't have anything to contribute to a conversation other than caregiving. I didn't want to complain and burden them with my sorrows, but I also didn't know if I had the capacity to listen to any of theirs, either. My life was consumed with all-things-Mom, not to mention I was existing on only a few hours' sleep every night, resulting in MS pain. My friends were, and are, dynamic Christians and they not only understood, but their unceasing prayers continue to be a powerful part of my life today. Thank you, Jesus!

May 5

"And I will ask the Father, and he will give you another advocate to help you and be with you forever." **John 14:16 (NIV)**

My friend Tina, who I nicknamed 'Sparkles', sent me a picture of herself after a blood transfusion and more chemo. She looked rough. I told her Mom and I were praying for her every day and she texted back that she would visit us soon and was praying for us, too. I showed Mom her picture, not expecting her to remember who she was but she burst into tears saying Tina was one of her "favorite students" (she never taught her). I cried with her; she was inconsolable for quite a while. We prayed together and Mom was calm again; the memory of Tina's picture faded from her memory. Alzheimer's could be cruel, but in this instance, it was a blessing.

May 6

"That is why, for Christ's sake, I delight in weaknesses, in insults, in hardships, in persecutions, in difficulties. For when I am weak, then I am strong." **2 Corinthians 12:10 (NIV)**

After pushing Mom's wheelchair every day, I was in severe MS pain. The chair was portable but very heavy and I had to lift it over the doorframe to get it on the sidewalk. The handles were also too low so I had to stoop over to push it. As a result, I spent a day resting with a heating pad on my back. Mom was worried and repeatedly asked if she could help. Finally I asked her to bring me a bottle of water so she went to the kitchen. After a time I got up to check on her. She was in the kitchen looking confused, and asked, "Why am I in here?" We laughed, I hugged her and told her she already helped me. She was grateful for that.

May 7

"A gift opens the way and ushers the giver into the presence of the great."
Proverbs 18:16 (NIV)

My mother loved rocks. She collected them all her life, but never as intensely as the years she lived with me. The large window seat in her bedroom was completely filled with rocks, large and small, and now there were buckets and baskets of them all over her room. She picked up rocks outside of restaurants, at the duck pond with Lisa, but mostly in our own backyard rock gardens. But as much as she loved keeping them, she also loved giving them away. Anyone who came to the house, including repairmen, were invited to her room to choose a rock, or rather 'God's little blessing'. Those gifted rocks would become cherished reminders of Mom to many of her 'fans'. (And many were given away at her funeral.)

May 8

"Jesus answered, "My teaching is not my own. It comes from the one who sent me." **John 7:16 (NIV)**

I was up at 3 am helping Mom to the bathroom, my 'new normal' for the rest of her life. Sometimes I was able to go back to sleep, but other times I stayed awake praying and watching old movies until it was time to make her breakfast. This was also around the time when Mom began sleep talking, usually about teaching. I transcribed many of her dreams, writing what she said verbatim. It was fascinating to hear her talking to her students, sometimes answering their questions. She was truly a gifted teacher and talked about going back to teach again until almost the very end. God gave her a special and rare gift for reaching high school students; Lisa and I were blessed to have been students of 'Mrs. Brown'.

May 9

"He is the radiance of the glory of God and the exact imprint of his nature, and he upholds the universe by the word of his power. After making purification for sins, he sat down at the right hand of the Majesty on high,"
Hebrews 1:3

It was a gorgeous but hot day for a Walk and Roll. I gave Mom a straw hat with a big white silk bow to keep the sun off her face. Turning the corner on our way home she saw something sparkly in the trees and, using her 'conducting' stick, she pointed it out to me. It looked like someone had strung sparkle lights all over the trees, but it was just the way the sun happened to be playing with the leaves and shadows. It was stunning, extraordinary. As I rolled her past, the lights continued to dance and sparkle. I prayed aloud, thanking God for our walks, and all the special little blessings He showed us along the way.

May 10

"Humble yourselves, therefore, under God's mighty hand, that he may lift you up in due time." **1 Peter: 5-6**

No matter how hard I tried, Mom was not doing well. I served her lunch on the patio and we got some of her favorite Andy's custard, but she never perked up. Breathing treatments, oxygen, and pain medication didn't help, nor did a wheelchair walk. While some days it took very little to keep her happy, other times (like this day) nothing worked at all. Instead of struggling and worrying, I had to learn when to throw up my hands, smile, and pray: "Thank you, God, for being with us today. I've done all I can as a human; please take over for me while I rest. Amen."

May 11

*"Let everything that has breath praise the Lord.
Praise the Lord."* **Psalm 150:6**

Mom was very confused at breakfast, asking if all her clothes had arrived yet. I didn't know what she was talking about and when I asked, she didn't know either. Lisa and I noticed something was "off" with her lately, and I suspected it was a UTI. Before the nurse arrived we went on our afternoon walk and roll and it was a huge hit. Most days she didn't remember the walks at all which was fun because it was a brand-new treat for her, over and over. The entire first half of our walk she prayed aloud, praising God, and so did I. And I silently prayed thanks for the wheelchair, too; it truly opened up the world for both of us.

May 12

"So teach us to number our days that we may get a heart of wisdom."
Psalm 90:12

The notes written in my daily devotional provided a sort of 'time capsule' of caregiving. From this day in 2019 I wrote, "Mother's Day with Mom, feeling so drained." In 2020, "Now Mom lives with me and she's very sick with another UTI infection. I'm no longer overwhelmed and afraid because of my dependence on Christ." In 2021 I wrote, "Back to feeling drained and burned out with Mom, exhausted. She needs so much. Praying always." But then in 2023: "Mom is gone. My focus is now on being a better Mom to my kids, sister to Lisa, and grandmother to little Charlie. Amen." Time goes fast. I got through it all—and you will, too, with God guiding you.

May 13

"We who are strong have an obligation to bear with the failings of the weak, and not to please ourselves." **Romans 15:1**

Around 4:30 am Mom was coughing badly. I checked on her and she told me she had a bad dream about someone wanting to lock her up. (I heard her sleep talking about this the night before, too.) I put her on oxygen and propped her up; it helped but in an hour she was coughing again. It sounded like bronchitis but no fever. Later that morning I thought it might be fun for her to go outside and blow bubbles on the patio. Unfortunately I hadn't considered how much energy and breath it would and she started coughing again…so no more bubbles. During times of constant frustration, struggle and strife, Romans 15:1 helped more than ever.

May 14

"Whoever is patient has great understanding, but one who is quick-tempered displays folly." **Proverbs 14:29**

Our cousin Preston drove from Dallas to visit. We were happy to see him but as always, Mom got mad when he talked to anyone but her. He asked me about something random and Mom loudly told Lisa, "When people their own age are talking she shouldn't interrupt." Mom apparently didn't realize that Preston was my age, not hers. Sadly she was always like this when anyone came to the house, whether family, friends, nurses or repairmen. It was frustrating, but I prayed for patience and understanding and tried to defer all the talk to her. It was a test of wills, and one I had to lose.

May 15

"And walk in the way of love, just as Christ loved us and gave himself up for us as a fragrant offering and sacrifice to God." **Ephesians 5:2**

Around 2 a.m. I was helping Mom to the bathroom when she had a coughing fit and struggled to breathe. I had a flash-back to the years when Jason had horrible asthma, also fighting to breathe. I felt as helpless then as I did now and found myself involuntarily trying to breathe for her. Mom kept saying 'I'm fine, I'm fine', I think trying to comfort us both. I stayed until she was calm enough to sleep then went back to my room, listening to the monitor. I knew it would only get harder and prayed for miracles, for strength, and to remain free from that devil, fear. I also praised Jesus for being on this path with us. No matter how difficult, we were never alone.

May 16

"So that I may come to you with joy, by God's will, and in your company be refreshed." **Romans 15:32**

Lisa always had a fun relationship with Mom. One night for dinner she made a healthy Spanish-style dish using cauliflower rice which Mom claimed she used to eat as a child. "No you didn't," Lisa said, "they didn't have cauliflower rice in the 1930's." Then Mom launched into a very mom-like story. "It was sad," she said. "We ate some of it and gave the rest away." Lisa challenged, "Who did you give it to?" Mom said, straight-faced, "To the tobacco people. They turned the rice into cigarettes. People liked to smoke them while they were working in the tobacco company." Lisa said, "I don't believe that." Mom said, "Well, they weren't very good cigarettes..." We all burst out laughing. God gave us a very good night.

May 17

"But I, with shouts of grateful praise, will sacrifice to you. What I have vowed I will make good. I will say, 'Salvation comes from the Lord.'
Jonah 2:9

My neurology appointment was frustrating when I learned I had more lesions on my spinal cord. I told the doctor about my clumsiness, tripping and bruising, the lack of sleep and constant wheelchair lifting. She suggested pain and sleep medications but I explained I had to stay somewhat alert day and night. Her strongest recommendation was 3 days of steroid infusions, but that would involve a hospital stay, which I couldn't do either. For now, I had to handle things as best I could and let God take care of the rest, as I knew He would.

May 18

"Let your reasonableness be known to everyone. The Lord is at hand; do not be anxious about anything, but in everything by prayer and supplication with thanksgiving let your requests be made known to God."
Philippians 4:5-6

It was a long day of appointments so I took Mom shopping. Things were going well at first but she got cranky when we had to wait for lunch. Then in the car she started asking why she couldn't drive. I played her favorite songs but she was sullen and angry all the way home. This was the beginning of a new 'toddler' phase for Mom; she was fine if she was fed and rested on time, but if anything was off she would spiral pretty fast. I prayed constantly for extra patience and kindness. Life is all about balance, but sometimes it's not so easy to achieve.

May 19

"As iron sharpens iron, so one person sharpens another." **Proverbs 27:17 (NIV)**

Every year I cover the Happy Trails Film Festival in Roanoke, Virginia. My dear friend, Dr. Fred Eichelman, is the creator of this wonderful event and it's one of my favorite things to do all year. Lisa took over and handled everything until I got home. Mom hugged me and asked if I had 'fun with my friends''. I gave her the gifts some of them gave her: a box of chocolates from Francine Locke, Dreama Denver's newest book signed 'to Beautiful Lou', and more. She happily looked at her goodies, confused why people she didn't know would do such a thing. "They're Christians, that's why," I told her. And then I heard the wheezing, and she started coughing…It was time to get back to work.

May 20

"I will instruct you and teach you in the way you should go; I will counsel you with my loving eye on you." **Psalm 32:8**

One of our favorite nurses, Leslie, checked on Mom and brought us portable oxygen tanks in case we needed to go somewhere. So after Leslie left I thought it would be fun to take Mom to a peach orchard for a nice outing. I was wrong. The drive was longer than expected and the small tank didn't hold enough oxygen for a round trip. By the time we got to the farm Mom was already tired and frustrated and wanted to go home. This was to be one of the last long-distance car trips with her... Our world was getting smaller; I prayed for comfort and peace for all of us.

May 21

"And the Lord said, "If you had faith like a grain of mustard seed, you could say to this mulberry tree, 'Be uprooted and planted in the sea,' and it would obey you." **Luke 17:6**

Late one night I heard Rev. T.D. Jakes talking about when his mother was dying of Alzheimer's and he had to take her off life support. His son said, "Daddy, you're so strong" but Rev. Jakes said he "never felt so weak". I understood. Sometimes I posted on social media how I was struggling or how weak I felt and was surprised when people called it "strength". As Rev. Jakes said, "That only looks like strength because they don't see the bleeding in your soul. And I was bleeding the next 20 years of my life." But it is faith in Jesus that saves us. "Faith rises up in spite of feelings and it does what it has to do and it responds to life however life goes at you."

May 22

"Lord, you give light to my lamp. My God brightens the darkness around me." **Psalm 18: 28 (NCV)**

My high school friends Kim and Corky came to the house unannounced. Mom was their former teacher and they knew we'd been having a rough month. "Come outside, Mrs. Brown, we have a surprise for you," Kim said. Mom hobbled out and saw their new "Slingshot" 3-wheeled vehicle in the driveway. She laughed and clapped, then Corky took her by the arm and led her to the car. It was a struggle, but once he got her inside she looked like a little girl, laughing joyfully as they drove down the road. When they got back Mom was still clapping and laughing. I thanked God profusely for the friends who knew to come see us, even when I repeatedly said no. Sometimes our friends know what's best even when we don't.

May 23

"God is the one who saves me; I will trust him and not be afraid." **Isaiah 12: 2 (NCV)**

We live in an area where straight-line winds, similar to tornadoes, can sometimes uproot giant trees out of the ground and destroy houses. I was consumed with worry about the large oak trees in our yard, thinking they might fall on the house. For weeks I worried about the "what if's" about those trees and then while praying I remembered what Dad always said: "If you have a million 'what ifs' in one hand and a nickel in the other, what do you have?" I finally called a tree expert who assured me our trees were healthy and well-rooted. He trimmed a few of the larger limbs and all was fine. Bottom line, it's the 'what ifs' in life that get you, and sometimes all it takes to eliminate them is to pray and act.

May 24

"Gray hair is like a crown of honor; it is earned by living a good life."
Proverbs 16:31 (NCV)

Shampoo day with Mom was a favorite for both of us. Because she couldn't go to a beauty shop anymore, her beautiful silvery gray hair was longer and thicker than it had ever been. She loved being pampered and I enjoyed making her happy. Thankfully she was still able to bend over the kitchen sink so I could wash and rinse there, while she held a towel over her eyes and nose. Next she'd sit in her wheelchair singing gospel songs while I blow-dried and styled her hair. The final step was rolling her chair to the full-length mirror and showing her how pretty she looked. Every single time to the very end, she said, "It's beautiful! How much do I owe you?" I miss the days that were simple yet filled with God's grace.

May 25

"If you are struggling to do good, no one can really hurt you. But even if you suffer for doing right, you are blessed."
1 Peter 3: 13-1 (NCV)

I had a doctor's appointment and thought it would be quick so I left Mom alone. When I got home I found her crying, terrified. Lisa's cat, Supercat, was sitting near her, also crying in distress. I forgot to leave a note, so Mom forgot where I was going. I hugged her, praying and feeling terrible. I brought her a cup of Blue Bell ice cream and very soon she was fine; she forgot everything. But I beat myself up until I prayed for help, asking Jesus to lift me above pain I couldn't control. Instantly, it was gone. I had some ice cream, too. God is so good, all the time.

May 26

"Make your father and mother happy; giver your mother a reason to be glad." **Proverbs 23: 25 (NCV)**

In addition to her rocks, books were Mom's biggest passion. When we were still going out regularly she bought stacks of inexpensive books at estate sales or anywhere she could get them. She rarely read more than a few pages, and in the end she forgot how to read. Still, her collection continued and between books and rocks, it was becoming dangerous to walk around her room. In addition to periodically dumping buckets of rocks in the backyard, I also started donating boxes of books. This had to be done stealth-like, with Lisa distracting her while I hauled everything out of the house. She never knew the difference and remained blissfully happy surrounded with her favorite things. Praise God.

May 27

"Pray continually and give thanks whatever happens."
1 Thessalonians 5:16 (NCV)

One of the strangest things I noticed about Alzheimer's was that both my parents eventually forgot different types of food. The first thing to go for Mom was her all-time favorite, guacamole. She didn't remember "avocados" and after trying a bite of guacamole she said she hated it. It was the same with other foods, like pizza. Who forgets pizza? But the one thing Mom never forgot was that before every meal, the three of us would hold hands and pray together. Even if she didn't know what she was eating, she always knew to thank the Provider of our meals. When everyone and everything left her mind, Mom's relationship with Jesus Christ stayed with her to the very end.

May 28

"I will always sing about the Lord's love; I will tell of his loyalty from now on." **Psalm 89:1 (NCV)**

Many local business owners loved Mom, too. Robbie and Tracy Shoults of Bear Creek Smokehouse treated Mom like a rockstar every time we visited. When she wasn't able to travel anymore, they came to our house to see her. Restaurant owner Nan Tomboni offered to bring us food many times, and our dear friend Johnny Horne, who died way too soon, never let anyone in my family pay for anything at his Cajun-Tex restaurant. And my beautiful Tina Bryan owned several restaurants and continually brought us food and baked good. Tina also died too soon. God brought us these friends who blessed us even while they were having difficulties in their own lives. I will never forget their kindness.

May 29

"In all the work you are doing, work the best you can. Work as if you were doing it for the Lord, not the people." **Colossians 3:23 (NCV)**

Mom had a terrible night and morning, wheezing with a dry, hacking cough while clutching at her chest in pain. After doing everything in my ability to help her, I prayed for God to help me remain in the present and not to 'time travel' into the future. It was painful to imagine how much worse this was going to get. Would I be capable of handling everything? How would I know what to do? God helped me remain focused on what I could do in the present and not worry about what was to come. For now, my job was to keep Mom as comfortable and pain-free as possible. God had guided me this far; I knew He would continue to lead and light the way.

May 30

"So we do not give up. Our physical body is becoming older and weaker, but our spirit outside us is made new every day. We have small troubles for a while now, but they are helping us gain an eternal glory that is much greater than the troubles. We set our eyes not on what we see but on what we cannot see. What we see will last only a short time, but what we cannot see will last forever." **2 Corinthians 4: 16-18 (NCV)**

My mother was exhausted from coughing and trying to breathe day and night. As a result, neither of us were sleeping much at all. Even her favorite Andy's custard couldn't help anymore. I wrote in my journal, "Heartbreaking. I can't fix this." During some of those darkest times, when frustration and fear were creeping in, I read the above scripture from 2 Corinthians. It comforted me more than almost any other passage in the bible.

May 31

"The aim of our charge is love that issues from a pure heart and a good conscience and a sincere faith." **1 Timothy 1:5**

For the first time in her life, Mom started losing hair. Lots of it. Handfuls were coming out after her shampoos, but I was able to style and fluff it so it wasn't noticeable and still very pretty. I was giving her regular pedicures now, too; she loved being pampered and always showed off her colorful toenails to her nurses. I tried to keep her world as normal and balanced as possible, filling the house with music and laughter. She and Lisa watched 'Little House on the Prairie' every night. We did our best, and that's all God expected of us.

June

"Train up a child in the way he should go; even when he is old he will not depart from it."
Proverbs 22:6

June 1

"Therefore, as we have opportunity, let us do good to all people, especially to those who belong to the family of believers." **Galatians 6:10 (NIV)**

Dr. Fred wrote a wonderful series of children's books about a cat named "Chatool" who witnessed the birth of Jesus. Mom adored the series and Fred even mentioned her in the credits. She never understand why, but it made her happy. He sent her a stuffed "Chatool cat" in the mail and when she opened the box she burst out crying. Hugging it tightly she asked, "Why am I getting such a special gift?" She never put it down the rest of the day and made sure I placed it at the foot of her bed at night. The kindness of our friends was one of the biggest blessings God gave us; it helped keep that darkness at bay.

June 2

"Where there is strife, there is pride, but wisdom is found in those who take advice." **Proverbs 13:10**

I tried to take Mom outside for a walk without her wheelchair for a little exercise. She'd been sitting so much and exercise was always my way of healing. But she barely made it to the street in front of the house when she started wheezing badly and told me her hips were hurting. I ran to get her wheelchair and rolled her back inside, followed by a breathing treatment. She was on oxygen the rest of the evening. Later her nurse reminded me that Mom was nearing the final stages of COPD; even simple exercise could hurt more than help now. That night I prayed for my mindset to change as needed, and to help me continue riding whatever waves were headed our way.

June 3

"The Lord does great things; those who enjoy them seek them." **Psalm 111:2 NCV**

I dreamed that I went to an Italian-style villa to visit my friend Tina. As I entered the room I saw her, looking beautiful and healthy. She was surrounded by a large group of people but when she saw me she ran over to me laughing, arms open wide. We hugged and cried together, and I told her how much I loved and missed her. She said the same. The dream seemed so real that I texted her about it. For the first time, she didn't respond. Later that day, her husband, Tim, posted on Facebook that Tina was on hospice; the chemo wasn't working and she was declining fast. I thanked God for my dream; I believe He allowed me to see Tina whole again, happy, with no pain. Thank you, Lord, for such a beautiful gift and friend. Amen.

June 4

"When you talk, do not say harmful things, but say what people need— words that will help others become stronger. Then what you say will do good to those who listen to you." **Ephesians 4:29**

Mom woke up singing 'Oh What a Beautiful Morning', and yes, it was. We had a lovely wheelchair walk around the block and everything was well until a hospice Chaplain came over. He was very nice, but he'd been to the house once before and stayed a little too long. Mom said she felt he didn't necessarily talk "to" us as much as "at" us. This visit triggered something dark inside my mother. She not only complained about his visit for hours after, until the very end of her life if anyone came to the door she said, "If it's that man again, tell him we don't want any," meaning the Chaplain…

June 5

"Here is a trustworthy saying: If we died with him, we will also live with him." **2 Timothy: 2:11**

Tina died. I knew it was coming but it was still very difficult. I told Mom and she was sad, as usual thinking Tina was one of her former students. She always remembered Tina when I described her as our "bald friend who owned the bakery". After helping Mom with her grief, I had to tamp down my own. I couldn't cry around Mom; she wouldn't understand and couldn't remember anything from one moment to the next. So I had to pretend things were normal and waited until Lisa came home from work so I could go to my room and break down, cry, and pray, thanking God for my Tina, who brought me (and everyone who knew her) such immense joy.

June 6

"May the Lord direct your hearts into God's love and Christ's perseverance." **2 Thessalonians 3:5**

Nurse Heather said she heard "crackling" in Mom's lungs but not enough to warrant antibiotics yet. This was frustrating because I was giving Mom three breathing treatments a day and kept her on oxygen almost constantly and still, crackling. Heather assured me I was doing everything right, but said things were eventually going to get worse no matter what we did. Meanwhile my friend Francine sent me a giant water bottle to make sure I stayed hydrated; she was worried about me and followed up with a phone call. She knew I couldn't cry in front of Mom so she made me laugh instead. God was holding me up, surrounding me with wise counsel, and making sure I wasn't alone.

June 7

"Truly my soul finds rest in God; my salvation comes from him."
Psalm 62:1 (NIV)

For months my usual routine was waking up at 3 a.m. to help Mom and after that, no more sleep for me. I did all the grocery shopping, made all the meals, dealt with all of the household things, and at the same time I was dealing with my own MS issues. One night for a shortcut I heated a frozen meatloaf, made Minute rice and salad the way Mom always made it with chopped lettuce, diced onions, tomatoes, salt and pepper. Out of all the meals I'd made from scratch, this was by far her favorite. She acted like I was Gordon Ramsey. What I learned was to stop trying so hard and to remember to BE STILL and know Who was really running our household.

June 8

"Not many of you should become teachers, my brothers, for you know that we who teach will be judged with greater strictness." **James 3:1**

For years Mom talked about going back to teaching, so Lisa asked her elementary teacher friend to give Mom some papers to grade at home. Unfortunately the stress of her "new job" made things worse. Mom woke up several mornings completely disoriented asking me to help her get ready for school, convinced she was supposed to go there to grade papers. I told Lisa how nervous it made her so we called it off. When I told Mom her job had ended she was relieved, but then worried that Lisa would get in trouble because she got fired. We prayed about it and she felt much better. "Grading papers was the only part of teaching I never liked anyway," she said, shrugging. Ah, Mrs. Brown...

June 9

"Whoever is slow to anger is better than the mighty, and he who rules his spirit than he who takes a city." **Proverbs 16:32**

Whenever Nurse Heather visited I'd give her a quick update and then turn it over to Mom. But this time Mom was very possessive of every moment. If Heather tried to talk to me about anything Mom diverted by showing off her puzzle book or asking her to write down her name and phone number, anything to make her stop talking to me. When nothing else worked she asked Heather to come to her room and pick out anything she wanted from her jewelry box (Heather rightfully said 'no thank you'). For whatever reason, Mom was mad at me all day. I prayed to God for extra patience; some days I needed boatloads of it…

June 10

"God is fair; he will not forget the work you did and the love you showed for him by helping his people. And he will remember that you are still helping them." **Hebrews 6:10**

After her bout with Covid in January, Mom barely weighed 90 pounds. I fed her as much as possible to help get her healthy again, but now she was overweight (possibly too much Andy's custard). Her knees and back hurt and some of her clothes didn't fit. When I expressed concerns, hospice reminded me that just like exercise, "dieting" shouldn't be on our agenda anymore. That's when a heartbreaking light finally came on for me: No matter how hard I tried, these were Mom's final months. She should eat whatever made her happy, and I needed to make sure she was comfortable and safe. As her caregiver and daughter, it was the best and most I could do from now on.

June 11

"We also have joy with our troubles, because we know that these troubles produce patience." **Romans 5:3 (NCV)**

When I came to Mom's room to help her to breakfast she wasn't sure who I was, or rather who she was to me. Whenever this happened, it was almost easier to think she was making it up, or even trying to hurt me, than to believe she really didn't know who I was anymore. But it was always the opposite—she simply didn't know. In spite of how I felt inside, when she asked who I was I always smiled broadly and said, "I'm Ann-Marie and you're my mama." Eventually her fog would clear. And still, no matter how hard I prayed, it always hurt just a little.

June 12

"The Lord's blessings bring wealth, and no sorrow comes with it." Proverbs 10:22 **(NCV)**

Mom and I had been putting jigsaw puzzles together since I was a little girl. I remember watching her doing puzzles with my grandparents, anxious for the day when they finally let me place a piece myself. Now, I found myself dreading the day when she couldn't do them anymore and prayed about it, knowing I'd miss that part of our life. As her disease progressed, she lost almost everything she'd known before. For now, I thanked the Lord we still had our puzzles to share together.

June 13

"The poor and needy look for water, but they can't find any. Their tongues are dry with thirst. But I, the Lord, will answer their prayers;" **Isaiah 41:17 (NCV)**

Our town was having issues with the water supply so people were scrambling to get bottled water. While Mom and I were on our wheelchair walk we saw a neighbor loading cases of water on their truck. He asked if we'd like some water and I held up my bottle and said 'no thanks'. He replied, "No, ma'am, I meant could y'all use a case of water--we have a truckload." I thanked him profusely and said yes. By the time we finished our walk there were two cases of water on our doorstep. Mom told Lisa all about the 'nice water man' at dinner and repeatedly asked, "Why is God so good to us?" He certainly was (and is).

June 14

"But if we hope for what we do not see, we wait for it with patience."
Romans 8:25

Mom slept late after a very bad night of coughing. When she finally got up I took her to a drive-thru for burgers. It was only a short trip but by the time we got home she was coughing so hard she couldn't eat, struggling to breathe. I did all the usual treatments and medicines, everything I could to help her. Once her breathing was steadier I realized I had to make yet another life-change for her. We'd already stopped taking long car trips, and now even driving a few blocks was too far without oxygen. My prayer that night was that I would continue to bend and not break as I faced all of the changes and challenges ahead of us.

June 15

"So I will walk with the Lord in the land of the living." **Psalm 116:9**

My friends Cindy and Susan from the Virginia film festival were passing through town and wanted to stop by for a visit. I had to scramble with Mom, explaining who they were before they arrived (she never did understand). We had a great visit and they were wonderful with Mom, giving her a rock and newspaper from the Grand Canyon. In turn, Mom let all of them choose rocks from her room. Before leaving they invited us out for dinner but those days were gone for us. We said our goodbye and while cooking dinner, I watched Mom happily looking at her newspaper. I thanked God for such a nice time with my friends, and for getting to feel "normal" a little while.

June 16

"You, Lord, give true peace to those who depend on you, because they trust you." **Isaiah 26:3 (NCV)**

God had to carefully guide me through some of Mom's stranger conversations, especially when she told mixed-up stories about my childhood. The most difficult was when she told a hospice nurse about my biological father, Jerry (or 'Jessie' as she now called him). He died in a car wreck when I was five, but Mom told the nurse that some of her students found him that night. Then she looked at me and asked, "Didn't I marry one of those boys? I was dating one of the students at the time." The nurse saw my shocked face as Mom continued. "We lived in the woods and had to pull a wagon with all our stuff in it everywhere we went…"

June 17

"The Lord has mercy on those who respect him, as a father has mercy on his children." **Psalm 103:13 (NCV)**

Between stress, lack of sleep, and physical pain from lifting Mom's wheelchair every day, my MS symptoms were becoming an even bigger problem. My left hand was experiencing nerve damage and sometimes whatever I was holding would involuntarily get thrown across the room. Now, if I was holding something, like a coffee cup, I had to physically stare at my hand and tell my brain 'keep holding it' until I could set it down. Knowing there was nothing I could do about it for now, I praised the Lord instead. At least I was still pushing a wheelchair instead of sitting in one; everything else was manageable. Praise God.

June 18

"But I, with shouts of grateful praise, will sacrifice to you. What I have vowed I will make good. I will say, 'Salvation comes from the Lord.'"
Jonah 2:9

Mom spent a lovely afternoon with Lisa feeding the ducks at a nearby pond, their favorite thing to do together. When they got home Mom was wheezing so I gave her a breathing treatment, but she wanted to go back outside for a wheelchair walk. We got about halfway when the blue skies suddenly turned dark gray and we heard a loud roar of thunder. Rushing home, everything went dark and the three of us watched from the patio as rain began pouring down, lightning striking all around us. It was beautiful, but powerful. As we stood together Mom began singing in her hoarse but still lovely voice, *"Then sings my soul, my savior God to thee, how great thou art, how great thou art…"*

June 19

"If you talk a lot, you are sure to sin; if you are wise, you will keep quiet."
Proverbs 10:19 (NCV)

At lunch Mom talked about how she once had to hide her food from coworkers because they would steal it. I asked if this happened when she was a teacher and she said it was when she was 'in between jobs'. Pressing further, she said there were times when she was either "out in the desert' or 'overseas'. She was mixing up her life with Dad's Navy years, because Mom certainly never went anywhere on a boat. I should have known better, but I corrected her story and told her about her childhood as well as mine. She didn't believe a word I said, but after listening, she sat back, crossed her arms and said, "Honestly I wish I didn't have such a great memory sometimes…"

June 20

""You asked, 'Who is this that made my purpose unclear by saying things that are not true?' Surely I spoke of things I did not understand; I talked of things too wonderful for me to know." **Job 42:3 (NCV)**

Talking to Lisa about Mom's latest 'overseas' story, I was concerned about how to handle it. Lisa wisely suggested, "She's creating her own history now, since she's forgotten all of reality. She has to have something to hang onto." This made me realize that I had been trying to turn Mom back into who she was before, instead of accepting who she was now. And while her stories weren't real to us, they were very real to her. In a strange Orwellian twist, or perhaps God's continual grace, whenever we challenged Mom on one of her stories, she seemed convinced that we were the 'crazy' ones. Praying diligently.

June 21

"Sing praises to the Lord, you who belong to him; praise his holy name."
Psalm 30:4

I found Mom cleaning her own toilet, which broke my heart a little. I took over and while scrubbing I was overcome with sadness and started crying, something very rare for me. Later Mom was having trouble breathing and told me she was struggling with sadness, too. We prayed together for help, and then despite the heat I took Mom on a wheelchair walk. As always, Mom was instantly happy again and shared her joy by singing to the Lord. I told her to look up--there was a lovely heart-shaped cloud, the only one in the entire sky, and it was covering the sun for us. That heart cloud kept us just a little cooler and shaded the rest of our walk. Thank you dear Lord, for your little gifts that help lighten our loads. Amen.

June 22

"We must not become tired of doing good. We will receive our harvest of eternal life at the right time if we do not give up." **Galatians 6:9**

After breakfast Mom said she was cold from the air conditioning so we went outside on the patio. I watered the plants and, thinking it might make her laugh, I sprayed a little mist on her. She was furious. It was hot and she was already completely dry, but she didn't understand why I sprayed water on her and stayed angry long after we went inside. We were still in our pajamas so even as I was helping her put on her clothes I could hear her grinding her teeth. Finally after helping her into her living room chair and giving her oxygen, she apologized. "I was left alone out in the woods too long I guess," she said. I hugged her and thanked God for giving me extra patience and kindness that morning; I needed it.

June 23

"But God shows his love for us in that while we were still sinners, Christ died for us." **Romans 5:8**

This day was an anniversary for me in California, a day when I try to give myself extra grace. For almost 30 years, "family" didn't mean as much to me. I only visited my parents and sister once a year, if that. My son and daughter-in-law lived nearby but they didn't feel wanted in my life at the time. So I lived somewhat isolated until I was called to follow God's path instead of my own. I thank Him every day that I moved to Texas to care for the people who needed me most. As a result, I gained a beautiful relationship with my parents, my son and daughter-in-law, and now two new grandchildren. Most of all, I now have a deeper relationship with Jesus Christ. So while I still feel some sadness on this day, I'm happier than I've ever been in my life. Praise God.

June 24

"Do not be interested only in your own life, but be interested in the lives of others." **Philippians 2:4**

Mom was up most of the night and early morning. Around 2:30 a.m. I heard her strange noises coming from her room. I went to check; her lights were on and she was sitting up. "I had a cookie," she said happily, wide awake, "and now I'm ready to go back to sleep." No more daytime naps for her. She started coughing so I gave her a breathing treatment and oxygen and then she finally fell asleep. Unfortunately I didn't, but I smiled as I offered praise to God, remembering how happy that cookie made her.

June 25

"Mercy, peace, and love be yours richly." **Jude 2**

It was a summer full of watching 'new old movies'. Mom didn't remember any of the classics anymore so we started with 'The Wizard of Oz'. She recognized the song 'Over the Rainbow' but didn't remember any of the storyline so Lisa and I enjoyed seeing her pure, childlike reactions. Later, Lisa and I talked about how this was maybe part of God's mercy, that the only 'good thing about Alzheimer's was that Mom got to experience regular old things in such lovely, brand-new ways.

June 26

"Remember that you will receive your reward from the Lord, which he promised to his people. You are serving the Lord Christ." **Colossians 3:24 (NCV)**

Lisa worked every day until 6 (or later) and liked to sleep late on weekends, so I rarely had any time on my own. I tried to get up an hour earlier than Mom, usually around 7 a.m., but then she started getting up at the same time. After praying for patience and compassion, I learned that in this season of my life I simply couldn't have any real "time off". And each time I prayed about it I was also reminded how blessed I was to be given such a beautiful yet complicated period of time with my family. This new job, as well as my life, was important now. Praise God.

June 27

"Let the heavens be glad, and let the earth rejoice; let the sea roar, and all that fills it; let the field exult, and everything in it! Then shall all the trees of the forest sing for joy" **Psalm 96:11-12**

It was 91 degrees, not hot at all for a Texas summer so I decided to risk a car trip and take advantage of the "cool streak". I somehow managed to hoist Mom's wheelchair and oxygen tanks into the car and drove her to the local arboretum. She absolutely loved our day there, 'oohing and ahhing' at the flowers and water features, enjoying every turn and trail. I sent pictures to Lisa at work which made her happy, too. When we got home, for the first time she didn't argue as I helped her in the shower to cool her down. And for the rest of the evening she thanked God for her "wonderful day".

June 28

"Do not worry about anything, but pray and ask God for everything you need, always giving thanks." **Philippians 4:4**

Feeling confident after our trip to the arboretum, I took Mom to lunch at a restaurant near our house. Everything was fine until she started coughing so bad we had to leave. By the time we got to the car she struggled for breath, and even the portable oxygen tank didn't work; she was too far gone. I drove fast to get us home where I gave her several breathing treatments, medication, and oxygen. Over an hour later, she was finally breathing normally but I was shaken. This had frightened me and I realized I couldn't take chances like that again; Mom needed to remain housebound. That night I got on my knees and prayed, grateful yet concerned about this next phase of life.

June 29

"For even the Son of Man came not to be served but to serve, and to give his life as a ransom for many." **Mark 10:45**

I talked to Lisa about how much smaller our worlds would become with Mom completely homebound. Months earlier, she was strong enough to walk entire stores an hour or so. Now, being away from oxygen and breathing treatments for even a few minutes could be dangerous. We knew Mom would be fine here forever but Lisa was mostly worried about me being isolated. We discussed having friends come over to give me a break, but other than her nurses Mom got nervous when anyone else came over now. While sadness sometimes hit me, I was deep in prayer and read my Bible and devotionals every night for strength and comfort. I would be fine. Mom was the priority; we had to keep her alive and happy as long as God allowed.

June 30

"With all humility and gentleness, with patience, bearing with one another in love," **Ephesians 4:2**

Nurse Leslie checked Mom and said her lungs sounded "very rough". She had bronchitis and her oxygen level was low, so Leslie ordered antibiotics. She also ordered a more portable wheelchair which became a huge blessing for me. It was lighter and much easier to maneuver, both inside and out. Meanwhile Mom was in a foul mood, upset that I was talking so much, and began telling Leslie about "that man" again, meaning the Chaplain who hadn't been to the house in over a month. It really was fascinating that she'd completely forgotten her husband of almost 53 years, but boy did she remember the sweet Chaplain who was in our house an hour or so. I prayed for extra patience; as always, I needed it.

July

"As each has received a gift, use it to serve one another, as good stewards of God's varied grace:" **1 Peter 4:1**

July 1

"Give your worries to the Lord, and he will take care of you." **Psalm 55:22 (NVC)**

Mom had a terrible night again, coughing and wheezing. By now we were fighting pneumonia with antibiotics and cough pearls and pain meds, and everything else in our arsenal. While rushing to plug in her oxygen machine I tripped and almost had a big fall, scaring both of us. My feet had been dragging from MS lately, especially my left side. Mom kept asking if I was okay and at the time I was, but later I was in pain from contorting my body against the fall. Usually when MS got this bad I needed steroid infusions to help but I didn't have time for that. I prayed for God to keep me strong. I was going to need it.

July 2

"Depend on the Lord and his strength; always go to him for help." **1 Chronicles 16:11**

I bought sparklers for the 4th of July including a few for Jason and Mimi. As I drove to their house I realized I was lost, in a completely different part of town. When I finally found their neighborhood I couldn't remember which was their house. I'd been there many times so it frightened me that I was so disoriented. My MS was flaring, but could I also have early onset dementia? It certainly ran in our family. After finding their house I dropped off the sparklers and headed home. I prayed, and remembering that fear is not from God I prayed for Him to take it all away and then thanked Him for always guiding me home...

July 3

"She looks well to the ways of her household and does not eat the bread of idleness." **Proverbs 31:27**

It was time to prepare Mom's bedroom for whatever was to come so Lisa stayed with her while I got busy. I prayed as I removed anything that wasn't absolutely necessary including useless pieces of furniture, never-to-be-read books, and estate sale knick-knacks. I organized her closet and dumped ten heavy buckets of rocks back in the yard. I cleaned the room top to bottom and hung new family pictures on the walls. When I was finished Lisa brought Mom in to see her 'new' room. She tearfully asked, "Do I really get to stay here?" and we both hugged her tight. Later that night I heard her happily singing 'Amazing Grace' in her 'new' room. Praise God.

July 4

"Be my place of safety where I can always come."
Psalm 71:3 (NVC)

I took Mom on a walk and roll early morning before it got too hot. Around the corner was a creek with weeds so tall you normally couldn't see the water, but someone had recently mowed it. Mom asked if we could walk the few hundred yards to look at the creek so I reluctantly led her over. She was so happy, clapping her hands at the water rushing below. But then she started wheezing. As I looked back at the wheelchair, it now seemed very far away. I prayed for help as I held her arm and waist tightly, guiding her back to the wheelchair. I pictured Jesus holding both of us--and as soon as Mom sat down she was fine. But this was one more thing off our list (along with the sparklers; she was terrified we would catch on fire..)

July 5

"But when he heard it, he said, "Those who are well have no need of a physician, but those who are sick."
Matthew 9:12

Nurse Heather was very concerned about Mom's cough. Antibiotics weren't helping and the next step was daily steroids, but the side effects of those could make her even worse. I continued giving Mom every breathing treatment possible but she was still struggling, moaning. "Don't be afraid of pain meds," Heather told me. "It's easy to forget how much physical pain your mother is experiencing from hours of coughing and trying to breathe." From then on, my prayers were directed toward discernment. I was now dealing with strong medication and needed to be fearlessly careful in knowing the best ways to help my mother.

July 6

"How good and pleasant it is when God's people live together in unity!"
Psalm 133:1

Mom woke up singing. It was such a beautiful way to start our day, but soon after the coughing began again. She felt better after getting a package from our Virginia friend Susan, an acrylic 'rock' with an angel etched inside. During her breathing treatment Mom started laughing while holding her angel rock. When I asked what was funny she said, "I just pictured you and Lisa fighting over my new rock when I die, so I'm keeping it in the coffin with me." She laughed so hard she could barely keep the breathing tube in her mouth. Praise God for the wonderful people and things that help us get through the darkness in the world.

July 7

"And he who searches our hearts knows the mind of the Spirit, because the Spirit intercedes for God's people in accordance with the will of God."
Romans 8:27 (NIV)

After washing Mom's hair I helped with her shower and then got her dressed. After so much activity she had another coughing attack, followed by the usual treatments. It had been a rough day. Mom was becoming increasingly fussy and not very nice to the point that I had to go around the corner to cry and pray for extra patience and kindness. No matter how hard I tried, nothing was helping her. Nothing. She was coughing and spitting day and night. I knew it was time for steroids, but it broke my heart. I prayed for Jesus to lift me above all of it; the load was far too much for me to carry alone.

July 8

"The night racks my bones, and the pain that gnaws me takes no rest."
Job 30:17

I was sitting on the floor finishing Mom's pedicure when my back hurt so bad I thought something had ruptured. While her polish was drying I went to my room, took a muscle relaxer and lay on my heating pad. But then I heard Mom yelling. "Ann-Marie! Ann-Marie! Come here!" I ran as fast as the pain would let me. "Where were you? You left me all alone!" She was angry. Instead of praying first, I snapped back, telling her I was in pain and giving her a laundry list of all the things I'd already done that morning, including laundry. We both apologized, and I assured her I wouldn't leave her alone anymore. As she napped in her chair I prayed for healing, for both of us…

July 9

"'And in the last days it shall be, God declares, that I will pour out my Spirit on all flesh, and your sons and your daughters shall prophesy, and your young men shall see visions, and your old men shall dream dreams;"
Acts 2:17

I woke up at 5 a.m. listening to Mom in the monitor "teaching" in her sleep. Her dreams were even more fascinating lately, sometimes teaching in a classroom, or coaching basketball, preaching in a church, or vividly talking to random people. My phone was (and still is) full of transcribed notes from her conversations, some long and detailed, some brief, funny, or downright strange. *"You're welcome to sit over here. You can turn the light on, it's right here. Do you want some ice cream? Just be careful don't rub it on your face, I'm in enough trouble."* Near the end her sleep talking became almost prophetic, with beautiful insight into what might be coming...

July 10

"But I am like an olive tree growing in God's Temple. I trust God's love forever and ever." **Psalm 52:8 (NCV)**

Nurse Heather came over to refill medications and reminded Lisa and me that when all else fails, we could give Mom a very low dose of liquid morphine from the box in the refrigerator. That box frightened us, but Heather explained that Mom's lung capacity was starting to dwindle and she would soon experience pain from simply trying to breathe. This was difficult to hear, but I thought of my elementary teacher Mrs. Caton saying, "Ignorance is bliss; don't be blissful." It was time to learn the hard stuff and overcome fears about those fridge meds. While Heather showed us how to administer each of them I prayed that we wouldn't need any of it anytime soon, while thanking God for His grace and love when we did.

July 11

"Praise the Lord! Praise God in his sanctuary; praise him in his mighty heavens! Praise him for his mighty deeds; praise him according to his excellent greatness! Praise him with trumpet sound; praise him with lute and harp! Praise him with tambourine and dance; praise him with strings and pipe! Praise him with sounding cymbals; praise him with loud clashing cymbals!" **Psalm 150: 1-6**

It was a frustrating morning; nothing was helping Mom. After she moaned that she was cold and "wanted to die", I put her in the wheelchair and walked her to the middle of the road. I stopped and told her to look up at the beautiful blue sky and the cathedral of trees draping over our street. She lifted her arms high as I began praying aloud, thanking God for our blessings and asking Him to help Mom through her horrible diseases. Mom wasn't cold anymore. Praise God from whom all blessings flow.

July 12

"The Lord will keep you from all harm—he will watch over your life; the Lord will watch over your coming and going both now and forevermore." **Psalm 121:7-8**

Lisa was happily coloring with Mom after her hospice visit so I walked outside with the nurse to talk. I needed to know exactly where we were with Mom's disease and she told me that Mom was "steady but declining"; both lungs were now rattly with fluid. "The best-case scenario," she said, "is your Mom might last the rest of the year, but probably no more than that." I somehow knew that was the case but hearing it so definitively was daunting. Lisa didn't have a monitor in her room so she never really knew how bad it was for Mom 24/7. So this time I prayed hard for Lisa before telling her the new information...

July 13

"I am with you and I will protect you everywhere you go" **Genesis 28:15**

At 4:30 a.m. I found Mom coughing in her closet, trying to open a diaper package. There were plenty in her dresser drawer but forgot where they were. I started putting them on the bathroom counter where she could easily find them, until the day when she couldn't do that for herself anymore either. I helped her all I could and she eventually settled down, but her lungs sounded especially rattly; I suspected pneumonia. I was very calm, unafraid; I knew Jesus was taking care of both of us every step of the way.

July 14

"He said to them, "Go into all the world and preach the gospel to all creation." **Mark 16:15 (NIV)**

Mom's cheeks were flushed red from steroids. Her appetite, which was already hearty, was now voracious. She constantly wanted cookies to the point that at dinner, like a toddler, I had to insist she eat her 'real food' first. The breathing treatments were increasing up to 4-5 per day, alternating between regular albuterol and Budesonide steroid. We needed Jesus in our home like never before so in addition to watching church on television, we also began watching "The Chosen" series together. Even without going to church, Jesus was definitely with us through scripture, prayer, gospel music, and now, even television.

July 15

"He must increase, but I must decrease." **John 3:30**

When Nurse Heather told me there were 'drawbacks' in giving Mom daily steroids I didn't know she meant towards me. Mom was driving me nuts, and I was having flashbacks of Jason's toddler years. Early one morning I heard loud sounds coming from her bathroom; she had opened the top of the toilet trying to fix a clog. I took care of that and noticed her toothbrush and comb were shoved down the sink drain, apparently trying to unclog that, too…As she watched me fixing everything she alternated between saying, "I'm bad" and apologizing with, "I didn't do it". I was running out of patience until I looked up at her with her hair wild, wearing a floral nightgown, smiling and shrugging. I laughed and hugged her. She had no idea. Thank you, Jesus, Amen.

July 16

"Observe what the Lord your God requires: Walk in obedience to him, and keep his decrees and commands, his laws and regulations, as written in the Law of Moses. Do this so that you may prosper in all you do and wherever you go." **1 Kings 2:3 (NIV)**

It was a very long day of cleaning, errands, and Mom-things. Lisa normally took over at night but she was late so I got Mom showered and into her nightgown. While hooking her up her oxygen tube I mentioned that I was tired. "What do you do all day to make you so tired?" she asked. I laughed but didn't want to explain. I told her MS makes me tired, which was the truth. We said our prayers together and she asked God to "help my Annie feel better". She was soon asleep. That night, I slept a while, too.

July 17

"For he satisfies the thirsty and fills the hungry with good things."
Psalm 107:9 (NIV)

Less than an hour after dinner Mom asked, "When's supper?" I was shocked and reminded her she'd already eaten her favorite meal of meatloaf, rice, peas, and she even had a huge cupcake for dessert. Not only did she deny eating dinner, but she also said, "I didn't get any lunch today either and I'm starving!" (Steroids.) So I took a chance, put her in the car and drove to Andy's Custard. The entire drive home she continued insisting she hadn't eaten all day. I finally said, "I'm so sorry Mom, I was too tired to cook today so we're only having ice cream for dinner tonight, is that okay with you?" She looked at her vanilla with strawberry custard, licked her lips, and said, "Fine with me!" Praise the Lord (and forgive me for the white lie)!

July 18

"Lord, answer me quickly because I am getting weak." **Psalm 143:7**

I woke up around 4:30 a.m. hearing Mom give a lecture to students about some type of drug they could take to "help them be better people". She woke up around 9 and I made her a hearty breakfast of pancakes. After that she went to her room so I did some work on my laptop. I thought she was in there reading but later she came out completely dressed and holding her purse, something I hadn't seen in months. "I thought we were going to town to eat lunch?" she said. It was barely 10 a.m. and I could hear her wheezing from across the room. She was out of breath from dressing herself, and then the coughing came. And that was that. I was already so tired but prayed for strength as I closed my laptop; it was time to get back to work.

July 19

"You did not choose me, but I chose you and appointed you so that you might go and bear fruit—fruit that will last—and so that whatever you ask in my name the Father will give you." **John 15:16 (NIV)**

I started writing my caregiving book soon after Dad died in 2020 and continued working on it during down-time with Mom. But as my caregiving duties increased and after deep prayer, I knew I had to set my writing aside. I tend to do really well when focusing on one project, but I've always had trouble trying to accomplish two important tasks at the same time. Either I was going to focus on that book, or I was going to properly take care of Mom, remaining alert and ready at all times. The answer was clear and once again, Jesus was directing all of my steps.

July 20

"But Jesus called them to him, saying, "Let the children come to me, and do not hinder them, for to such belongs the kingdom of God." **Luke 18:16**

Several of Mom's lifetime pleasures were ending. I cancelled her newspaper subscription when she couldn't read it anymore. And after a lifetime of drinking several pots of coffee a day she asked, "What is this horrible black stuff?" She never drank it again. Crossword puzzles went away next, something she worked on almost every day of her life. Lisa got her Seek and Find puzzle books and she enjoyed that for a while, but one morning I saw her staring blankly at a puzzle. "What am I supposed to do with this?" she asked. The only thing left were easy jigsaw puzzles and children's coloring books and crayons. Lord willing, she would have fun doing those--until she couldn't anymore.

July 21

"The night racks my bones, and the pain that gnaws me takes no rest."
Job 30:17

Mom was acting especially feeble. She told me her back hurt and she was afraid to walk for fear of falling. I put a pain patch on her back and gave her a pain pill but there was definitely something else wrong. She was forgetting things she usually remembered, once asking if she was ever a grandmother. And during lunch she repeatedly said, "Son of God, Child of God" to Lisa and me. She did that when she was in the hospital the year before after having an allergic reaction to an antibiotic. I arranged for hospice to come over first thing the next morning, and that night I stayed by her bed praying; she was in terrible pain, moaning until she finally fell asleep.

July 22

"God is our refuge and strength, an ever-present help in trouble." **Psalm 46:1 (NIV)**

God sent a wonderful new hospice nurse named Beverly to see Mom. After checking her vitals I told her everything that happened the day before. Beverly took Mom to the bathroom to test for a UTI and a few moments later she loudly exclaimed, "OH MY!" Turned out that Mom had a terrible infection. I wanted to cry but Beverly said, "Don't you dare blame yourself! With all your mother is going through no one could know whether it was COPD, dementia, oxygen or anything else. And she can't explain the difference between a sore back or painful urine. Do not blame yourself!" We hugged and prayed together. (Thank you, Jesus, for your good care and protection, and for holding our hand through those hardest times. Amen.)

July 23

"Rejoice not over me, O my enemy; when I fall, I shall rise; when I sit in darkness, the Lord will be a light to me." **Micah 7:8**

As if the week couldn't get crazier, Mom fell in the front yard and almost pulled me down with her. At the time we didn't know about the free 'Lift and Assist' service, so Mom had to lie in the grass quite a while waiting for hospice. Thankfully a neighbor saw us and helped get Mom up and into the wheelchair. He then rolled her into her bedroom and helped get her into bed. Mom hugged him and told him she loved him before he left. A hospice nurse arrived just as he was leaving; no injuries but she said we would both probably be sore the next few days (she was correct). It could have been so much worse but God was always there with us, catching us when we'd fall....

July 24

"Rejoice with those who rejoice, weep with those who weep." **Romans 12:15**

I couldn't sleep. My television was still on at 6 a.m.. when I heard Mom stirring in her room. I went in to check on her and she was sitting up in bed, looking happy. I ran over and hugged her then rushed to the kitchen to make her breakfast. Normally I had time before she woke up but now I scrambled to fix everything, drink some coffee and pray for the day. But what a glorious start, seeing her smiling for a change. She said her back hurt a little but she didn't know why. It could have been from the fall the day before or the UTI, or any number of things. But as I served my mother her breakfast, I said prayers of deep gratitude for such a simple and sweet morning.

July 25

"But godliness with contentment is great gain," **1 Timothy 6:6**

Mom was sleep-talking about being bored. This is part of what I transcribed: *"Newspaper on the table for breakfast, just waiting for time to pass most of the day. Boring. In the evening, we would watch the news, waiting for time to pass again. The next day it was the same. Realized how boring it was with nothing to do. In the evening we would make supper, maybe have a sandwich, peanut butter. Through the day, nothing changes. Boring."* I'm pretty sure she was talking about her last few years with Dad. We never watched the news here; her newspaper was long gone, and I've never had peanut butter in my house. I prayed that when she woke up, she would find peace and contentment in the life she was living in now.

July 26

"Put on the whole armor of God, that you may be able to stand against the schemes of the devil." **Ephesians 6:11**

It was a rough morning of coughing that continued through the rest of the day. During this time we were still eating dinner in the dining room together; it had become the most special part of the day for all three of us. But it was getting difficult for Mom to eat now; she was hungry and coughed between bites. That night I had to give her a breathing treatment at the table and realized it would be easier for her to eat her meals in her comfortable chair next to the oxygen tank. Sadly, that was to be our last time eating dinner at the table together. I suddenly felt like I was in a battle that I was too tired and ill-equipped to fight... so I prayed for the Holy Spirit to give me enough armor to power through.

July 27

"Carry each other's burdens, and in this way you will fulfill the law of Christ." **Galatians 6:2 (NIV)**

Mom was struggling to breathe even more than the day before. Her hospice nurse talked to me again about giving her low doses of morphine when things got this bad. I still hadn't done that; there was a part of me that felt I wasn't qualified to handle a medicine that was so strong, so 'scary sounding'. But she reminded me that most of Mom's daily meds were stronger than the amount of morphine I would be administering. And when she was in severe pain or distress it could help her more than the other medications. I agreed that if her last breathing treatment of the night didn't work I would do what was needed. And then I prayed and prayed for courage and discernment.

July 28

"Blessed be the God and Father of our Lord Jesus Christ, the Father of mercies and God of all comfort, who comforts us in all our affliction, so that we may be able to comfort those who are in any affliction,."
2 Corinthians 1:3-4

Around 10 p.m. I heard strange sounds coming from Mom's room and found her slumped over and asleep in her rocking chair. Knowing it would hurt her back I woke her up to put her to bed. Her eyes popped open and she asked, "Am I your grandma? Who is your daddy?" When I told her that my daddy was Jerry she said didn't know him and asked where he was. "He died," I said. She smiled and said, "Oh, I'm so sorry." I tucked her in bed, kissed her on the cheek and said, "I love you." And then I cried and prayed in my room the rest of the night.

July 29

"You yourselves like living stones are being built up as a spiritual house, to be a holy priesthood, to offer spiritual sacrifices acceptable to God through Jesus Christ." **1 Peter 2:5**

I heard banging in Mom's room again and found her putting the rocks displayed in her windowsill into a large basket. She said she wanted to make me happy by throwing them away. I was gutted. I hugged her and told her I loved her rocks and reminded her that we chose the house after envisioning her pretty rocks on that very windowsill. I added, "They won't be happy being thrown back out in the yard, right?" She agreed and I tearfully watched as she carefully put them back. That day on our wheelchair walk Mom prayed aloud, apologizing to God for 'almost getting rid of His rocks'…

July 30

"You also, be patient. Establish your hearts, for the coming of the Lord is at hand." **James 5:8**

It was an interesting day. Mom wanted to know the name of the store where we went earlier that day, "the place Lisa goes all the time, too." We hadn't been anywhere other than a walk around the block, but I named a few local stores we'd been to before. She was getting frustrated. "No, it's the place where we went inside and talked to that woman about doing that thing. She was going to Rio de Janeiro and I hope she didn't get killed there." I gave up and told her we didn't go to a store but she just laughed and gave me a 'bless your heart' look. I prayed for patience, realizing she was in her own world, not mine. But just in case I called Lisa and asked if she knew anyone going to Rio…

July 31

"Oh come, let us sing to the Lord; let us make a joyful noise to the rock of our salvation!" **Psalm 95:1**

Mom and I both slept until 8:30 a.m., miraculously late for both of us. I woke hearing her singing "Water, cool clear water". I played the song on Spotify and together we sang along, "Keep a movin' Dan don't you listen to him Dan…" The rest of the day was filled with gospel music and everything was wonderful until nighttime. Mom wheezed badly and at one point she got out of bed. I found her in the living room with her flashlight looking crazed. She said she needed her cane but it was beside her bed as always. I gave her a drink of water and put her back to bed with oxygen. And I thanked God for giving us both extra sleep and joy that day; it made the night easier to bear.

August

"Then the righteous will shine like the sun in the kingdom of their Father. He who has ears, let him hear." **Matthew 13:43**

August 1

"It is good to praise you, Lord, to sing praises to God Most High, It is good to tell of your love in the morning and of your loyalty at night."
Psalm 92:1-2 (NCV)

After coughing and struggling all night and morning, Nurse Heather arrived. Mom's oxygen was low and her lungs were 'cloudy' but so far it wasn't pneumonia. After treatments and meds Mom was exhausted even before breakfast. "I'm ready to go with Jesus," she told me, but I assured her it was just a rough morning and she'd be fine. After she ate she was still in pain so I gave her a low dose of morphine as Heather suggested. Later I said a prayer of gratitude as Mom fell asleep in her chair, still rasping but peaceful. I knew as hard as things were now they were only going to get worse, but God was with us, guiding the way.

August 2

"A happy heart is good medicine, but a broken spirit drains your strength."
Proverbs 17:22 (NCV)

It was a relatively easy day. Mom woke up singing gospel songs, breathing a little better. She was happily eating her favorite chicken meal when she suddenly became angry, ranting about not letting "that man" come to the house again (meaning the hospice chaplain). She was escalating and nothing I said helped, so I put on music to calm both of us. But then a song called 'Light in the Hallway' by Pentatonix played and I completely lost it. I helped Mom to her chair and broke down in the kitchen, just as Lisa came home. She found me leaning against a wall crying and without saying a word, she just hugged me while it played. I needed to cry and prayed thanks to Jesus for my sister.

August 3

"Not only that, but we rejoice in our sufferings, knowing that suffering produces endurance, and endurance produces character, and character produces hope, and hope does not put us to shame, because God's love has been poured into our hearts through the Holy Spirit who has been given to us." **Romans 5:3-5**

Mom and I entered a new season where sleep was almost completely ending for both of us. It still wasn't as bad as it would become, thankfully it was a slow progression. The routine began soon after putting her to bed when she fought to breathe. Her chest and throat were now burning from constant coughing and breathing treatments and she often said she wanted to die, was ready to be with Jesus. Nights were sad and frustrating so the best I could do was pray for her pain to ease, and mine, too.

August 4

"Then he prayed again, and heaven gave rain, and the earth bore its fruit."
James 5:18

Just when depression was beginning to set in for both Mom and me, there was a lovely summer rain shower. While moving plants out to get a good drink, the rain felt so soft and warm that I brought Mom outside, too. We sat on the porch awhile and then I had her stand out in the rain with me, telling her to look up at the sky. As the drops fell on our faces and ran down our necks we laughed, so happy. It was glorious. I prayed aloud thanking God for His glory and Mom added a loud, 'Amen!' Back inside we resumed breathing treatments and oxygen, but it was worth it. A few years later I would do the same thing with my grandsons. Thank you, dear God, for summer rain. Amen.

August 5

"A time to weep, and a time to laugh; a time to mourn, and a time to dance;" **Ecclesiastes 3:4**

It was shampoo day for Mom, and after styling her hair I set up our portable foot spa to give her a pedicure. I put a little extra bubble bath in the water, then ran to get the pedicure tools. When I got back Mom was laughing like a little girl because there was a 3-foot tower of soap foam climbing out of the foot spa, getting even higher until I turned it off. It was like an episode of 'I Love Lucy'. Mom and I laughed and laughed, until she started coughing. But she talked about that 'foam monster' the rest of the day and night. Thank you, Lord, for the beautiful moments of lightness and laughter.

August 6

"Every good gift and every perfect gift is from above, coming down from the Father of lights, with whom there is no variation or shadow due to change." **James 1:17**

Jason and Mimi were in the midst of putting their new store together so I took some much-needed time away from Mom to help. It was fun, mostly because I cherished any chance to spend time with them. Later that evening while celebrating Jason's birthday he surprised me with a gift: a gorgeous book about Disneyland. It meant more to me than he could know because we spent so many wonderful birthdays there together, both his and mine. And it was also a lovely reminder of my son's beautiful soul, giving me a gift on his own birthday. Sometimes I'm not sure who raised whom, but every day since August 6, 1985, I pray thanks to God for giving me such an incredible son.

August 7

"Train up a child in the way he should go; even when he is old he will not depart from it." **Proverbs 22:6**

I began cleaning and organizing our guest room; I was turning it into a nursery for my grandson, due in September. I'd been storing all the extra furniture pieces and random items from Mom's room in there so I either moved them to the shed or loaded them in the car to be donated. I was excited about being a grandmother and prayed Mom would be around long enough to experience her first great-grandson. What an incredible and ironic gift of life, at such a time when my mother was nearing the end of hers.

August 8

"So we do not lose heart. Though our outer self is wasting away, our inner self is being renewed day by day." 2 **Corinthians 4:16**

It was heartbreaking when Mom began losing her ability to read, asking the definition of simple words and phrases. This was especially difficult, considering she taught Lisa and me how to talk and read, and was also our favorite high school teacher. And then one day we were working on a collage jigsaw puzzle featuring famous book covers like 'Tom Sawyer' and 'Romeo and Juliet'. She didn't recognize any of them. I prayed harder than ever not to show emotion as I 'taught' my brilliant English Literature teacher/mother about Mark Twain, Hemingway, Shakespeare…

August 9

"Each of you should give what you have decided in your heart to give, not reluctantly or under compulsion, for God loves a cheerful giver." **2 Corinthians 9:7**

After dinner Mom and I went on a walk and roll. She marveled at the clouds, the pretty summer flowers and green grass, praising God for His goodness along the way. At home, she said she was hot and sweaty so I asked if she wanted a shower. Shockingly, she said yes and sang 'I'm in the Jailhouse Now' while showering. That night I said extra prayers of gratitude. I knew tomorrow might not be so good; that was the nature of our roller coaster life now, so high one day, then plummeting the next. But with Jesus and by His absolute Grace, I was ready for whatever came next.

August 10

"Therefore lift your drooping hands and strengthen your weak knees, and make straight paths for your feet, so that what is lame may not be put out of joint but rather be healed." **Hebrews 12:12-13**

I found a new "holistic" way to uncramp Mom's poor arthritic hand. The cramping caused her terrible pain, twisting her fingers so badly they would overlap. Each time this happened I would kneel down next to her, telling her to look me in the eyes as I gently massaged her hand. Then I'd suddenly either cross my eyes and make crazy faces or I'd yell loudly to startle her. Either way it made her laugh hard and her hand would instantly relax and un-clench. Every time. I'm not sure that's the actual "medical" way to help with a cramped hand, but it worked for Mom, and it always gave us a much-needed laugh, praise God.

August 11

"By wisdom a house is built, and by understanding it is established;"
Proverbs 24:3

Early one morning while Mom was still sleeping I rearranged the living room. God had prepared me for whatever was to come, and now it was time to prepare the house. Mom was now almost completely wheelchair bound, not only outside but inside, too. I needed to make more space throughout the house so I moved furniture around, including our very heavy couch. I removed rugs and anything that might get under the wheels. It was very difficult and I had to work fast (and quietly) but when I was finished, I felt at peace. Our house was prepared.

August 12

"And they devoted themselves to the apostles' teaching and the fellowship, to the breaking of bread and the prayers." **Acts 2:42**

Dinner was always a special time for the three of us. Growing up our family always ate at the dining table together beginning our meal with a prayer. We continued the tradition every evening for dinner, holding hands as Mom said the prayer. Her favorites were Lisa's street tacos, cauliflower pizza, or my "healthy" enchilada dinner. No matter what we ate, it was a time when we shared stories about our day, and we usually ended laughing hysterically. I thank God for those wonderful meals; I will cherish them forever and this tradition continues in my home today with my children and grandchildren.

August 13

"I long to see you so that I may impart to you some spiritual gift to make you strong— that is, that you and I may be mutually encouraged by each other's faith." **Romans 1:11-12**

Every few months I tried to spend some time with my friends. It was important for me in the same way a new mom needs to be around other "adults". My core group of friends offered laughter, perspective, and most of all prayer. They listened to me vent but not so much that it hurt. I didn't know at the time, but those hours and prayers spent with my friends helped build up my strength for everything to come. We continue to get together as often as possible despite busy schedules; I thank God constantly for such wonderful friends.

August 14

"A generous person will prosper; whoever refreshes others will be refreshed." **Proverbs 11:25**

Mom's appetite from the daily steroids was getting out of control. Moments after eating a meal she'd say, "I'm hungry, what's for supper?" Trying to convince her she'd already eaten rarely worked. Even if we showed her the crumbs still clinging to her shirt she'd just shrug, smile, and say, "My bad, what's for supper?" Sometimes Lisa and I could distract her, but more often than not we ended up fixing her another plate of food or gave her cookies and ice cream. Her nurses said there wasn't a solution to this other than just keeping her happy and comfortable. So since she wasn't diabetic we gave her whatever she wanted. And we doubled-up on our prayers…and groceries.

August 15

"Pray continually and give thanks whatever happens. That is what God wants for you in Christ Jesus." **Thessalonians 5:16-17**

Woke at 4:30 a.m. to Mom sleep-talking, or rather sleep-preaching, about being a "good Methodist" and loving God and Jesus. Soon after she was coughing and started to gag so I ran in to help and called hospice. After a checkup, Nurse Heather said Mom's right lung capacity was closing off and her oxygen level was low. She needed antibiotics again. The only good moment that morning was that Mom remembered Heather and asked about her 5 young boys. The steroids were maybe helping with her sharpness and even in pain, she seemed happy and energetic. I prayed gratitude for even a fraction of light during some of those darker days.

August 16

"A good man leaves an inheritance to his children's children, but the sinner's wealth is laid up for the righteous." **Proverbs 13:22**

Mom was in a great mood after sleeping until noon and a difficult night. She was still coughing and wheezing, but very happy. She asked me to bring one of her stuffed animals into the living room and said she wanted to give it to her new great grandbaby. But she suddenly began crying, saying she wished she had more to give. I was just happy she even remembered she was going to be a great-grandmother and I started crying with her. I hugged her and said getting to meet his great grandmother was a gift in itself. Then we prayed over her little gift, that it would bring joy to the baby.

August 17

"Go, eat your bread with joy, and drink your wine with a merry heart, for God has already approved what you do." **Ecclesiastes 9:7**

3:30 a.m. I had to change Mom's sheets, the first of many times to come. She was grateful and apologized as I helped her get back to bed, coughing so badly she could barely speak. After the usual treatments plus cough syrup she finally settled back to sleep. Around 6 a.m. I heard her sleep talking: "Breakfast, supper, and what comes in between?" then she laughed. She was always hungry now, even in her sleep so I made her a special breakfast of strawberry waffles and a banana. She ate every bite and was in such a great mood she wanted to go for a walk and roll. Praise God for difficult nights that turn into wonderful days.

August 18

"One generation shall commend your works to another, and shall declare your mighty acts." **Psalm 145:4**

I was at Jason and Mimi's house decorating their nursery until after midnight. It was so much fun, organizing and putting everything together, placing the forest animal murals I bought on one wall and the jungle and monkeys on another. They loved it and I was exhausted, but in a much lighter way than usual. This room was going to hold my first grandchild, the start of a new generation in our family. I was overwhelmed with gratitude to God; this child would bring endless love and light to all of us.

August 19

"For my iniquities have gone over my head; like a heavy burden, they are too heavy for me." **Psalm 38:4**

Even though Mom's lungs were still crackly and her oxygen level was lower than it should've been, her nurse said she didn't need antibiotics. I trusted her decision but watched over Mom closely. This made me think of my poor Dad, left alone in Memory Care without family being able to follow up on medications, or to make sure he was being treated well. Back then I had to blindly trust all the nurses, both staff and hospice, to make the right decisions for him. With Mom, I was with her almost every moment day and night, and when I couldn't be there Lisa was. Dad ended up with no one. I still pray for peace about this and will do so again, right now...

August 20

"Brothers, I do not consider that I have made it my own. But one thing I do: forgetting what lies behind and straining forward to what lies ahead,"
Philippians 3:13

I was getting ready for a rare night out when Lisa told me she needed to run a quick errand. After she left, Mom anxiously yelled out, "Lisa's outside waiting for you!" I told her Lisa already left but she yelled, "NO! She's outside waiting!" I prayed for patience as I led her to the carport to see that no one was there. Frustrated, Mom angrily said, "Okay then, I'll just pack my things and go." That's when I realized she was upset that I was going out without her. We talked about it and she admitted she missed me when I was gone. I gave her a cookie and assured her I'd be home soon and she was fine after that. But this is why I rarely left the house from then on.

August 21

"There will be a booth for shade by day from the heat, and for a refuge and a shelter from the storm and rain." **Isaiah 4:6**

I spent the day at Jason and Mimi's helping them clean and "nest" for the baby's arrival. After hours of working, I went out to lunch with Mimi's mother. It was wonderful talking to the "other grandma" about our upcoming grandson, and how all our lives would soon change. Just as we were leaving a sudden lightning storm hit. She had an umbrella and tried to cover me while we ran to our cars but the wind was blowing sideways. We were drenched, laughing all the way. As I drove home, I offered prayers of overwhelming gratitude for all the blessings God was pouring over my family. Life, even through the storms, was beautiful.

August 22

"This was to fulfill what was spoken by the prophet Isaiah: 'He took our illnesses and bore our diseases.'" **Matthew 8:17**

Nurse Heather was again concerned about Mom's lungs. They were crackling even more, her oxygen was too low, and she had a fever. It was another infection. Heather called in a strong antibiotic and stopped the daily steroid for a stronger 5-day dose to hopefully strengthen her lungs. As always, we were desperately trying to fight off pneumonia. And this also explained Mom's angry outbursts lately. Heather explained it could be from pain that she doesn't know how to express things, much like a toddler. I increased her pain meds dosage, and I also increased my prayers; the last thing any of us wanted was for Mom to suffer…

August 23

"Train up a child in the way he should go; even when he is old he will not depart from it." **Proverbs 22:6**

After lunch Mom was eating a cookie and told me she was happier than she'd ever been in her life. She thanked me for "letting her stay here" and I responded as I always did, thanking her for being here with Lisa and me. I told her we were honored to have our mama living with us and grateful that God brought us together in our wonderful home. She started crying so I hugged her and noticed she was hot. She had a mild fever so I gave her some Tylenol, but I would have to watch her very carefully the next few days.

August 24

"A disciple is not above his teacher, but everyone when he is fully trained will be like his teacher." **Luke 6:40**

I woke at 6 a.m. hearing Mom "sleep teaching" and preparing her new class for the upcoming year. This was fascinating because in her awakened state she had forgotten almost everything about teaching, including all her students, including favorites I never thought she'd forget. She didn't remember the schools or towns where she taught, but in her dreams, she was still the God-gifted "Mrs. Brown".

August 25

"I consider that our present sufferings are not worth comparing with the glory that will be revealed in us." **Romans 8:18 (NIV)**

All night and early morning Mom was agitated. She thought she had to go teach "over the mountain" and didn't want to disappoint her students. I was concerned she had sepsis, a bad reaction to the strong antibiotics, so Nurse Leslie came over. She was convinced it was pneumonia and called for a mobile x-ray. She gave mom a dose of pain meds and waited with us for the x-ray tech. Yes, Mom had pneumonia. That night I prayed by her bedside for a painless sleep, and I also prayed for Mimi as she was giving birth to my grandson in the nearby hospital. I so wanted to be two places at once; for now, I had to be with Mom.

August 26

"For the creation waits in eager expectation for the children of God to be revealed." **Romans 8:19 (NIV)**

My grandson was born at 6:21 a.m. When I arrived in the hospital Jason was holding him. He was so tiny, more blanket than baby, just a little squiggle of face and hands opening and closing, unsure of what to cling to. Mimi had a c-section so she was tired but overjoyed with this new life in our lives. I ran some errands for them, helped Mimi's mother feed their dogs and brought Jason some food. But then I talked to Lisa; she was stressed because the new meds were causing Mom to hallucinate. I had to rush home to meet with Nurse Leslie again, but all the way home I prayed, joyfully, for our many blessings both good and bad, happy and sad. All were important, and lessons, and life.

August 27

"Let everything that has breath praise the Lord. Praise the Lord."
Psalm 150:6

No matter how sick she got, whether it was Covid or pneumonia, Mom never stayed in bed. I made the living room as comfortable as possible for her and since she wasn't able to sit at the counter to work on our jigsaw puzzle, Lisa got her a coloring book and crayons. Mom and Dad once enjoyed coloring in the adult coloring books so we thought she might be insulted by the childish pictures. But she absolutely loved it and colored all day until evening when her fever rose over 100. Still, she never complained; I gave her meds and treatments and she continued to happily color. Praise God from whom all blessings flow.

August 28

"Blessed are the people to whom such blessings fall! Blessed are the people whose God is the Lord!" **Psalm 144:15**

I'd been awake since around 4 a.m. when I heard Mom saying loudly she was "freezing". I went to her room and she was wide awake, funny and alert so I asked if she was okay. "Well," she said, "I'm kinda hungry!" I gave her a cookie, turned off her ceiling fan and she seemed ready to go back to sleep. A few hours later I heard her stirring again; she was trying to turn the ceiling fan back on because now she was 'burning up'. I turned on the fan and brought her a coloring book and crayons. As I left to make breakfast she said, "I'm so happy I could cry!" I hugged her and said, 'Me, too, Mom." I thanked God because moments like that made up for the lack of sleep.

August 29

"Be joyful in hope, patient in affliction, faithful in prayer." **Romans 12:12 (NIV)**

While on a wheelchair walk Mom became confused and asked if she was my grandmother. She knew my name but didn't understand that she was my mother. Later she asked Lisa who her father was. Nurse Heather said her confusion was probably from a combination of Alzheimer's, COPD, pneumonia, and strong medications. I knew from MS that whenever I had any "extra" illness, like the flu or bronchitis, my symptoms were much worse, so I couldn't imagine what Mom was going through. Lisa and I both needed extra patience and kindness during those times and that's where my prayers were directed, non-stop.

August 30

"He has made everything beautiful in its time. Also, he has put eternity into man's heart, yet so that he cannot find out what God has done from the beginning to the end." **Ecclesiastes 3:11**

Mom was happily singing and talking all day. Whether it was from steroids or the constant prayer surrounding her, what a blessing. On our walk and roll she wanted me to pick a flower for her. As she was placing it in her hat I saw a turtle struggling to climb over the curb to get to the nearby woods. I picked it up and showed it to her, then we said a little prayer for our new friend as it scampered into the woods. Mom asked me to call Lisa to tell her about it and when she answered Mom said, "Annie got me a pretty flower for my hat!" The turtle had already disappeared from her memory forever, but the flower remained.

August 31

"Behold, I am the Lord, the God of all flesh. Is anything too hard for me?" **Jeremiah 32:27**

It was a good day; Mom was in a beautiful mood. While she was happily coloring, Lisa and I talked about how she seemed to be following the same progression of Dad's disease. Like Dad, after she stopped reading and watching television she took up coloring. Dad stopped coloring when he couldn't remember colors anymore; trees were purple, or clouds were brown. Then one day after staring at a picture blankly, brows furrowed, he said he had a headache and wanted to stop. He never colored again. For now, Mom was happy and on this day she thanked Jesus saying, "This is the best day of my life!" No matter what was to come, He was with us; we were never alone.

September

"He made the moon to mark the seasons; the sun knows its time for setting." **Psalm 104:19**

September 1

"He said to them, "It is not for you to know times or seasons that the Father has fixed by his own authority." **Acts 1:7**

At 5:02 a.m. I heard Mom on the monitor saying, "I want to see who's holding the baby. Where's the baby?" Next I heard her rattling around in the bathroom so I went in to check on her. She cheerfully said, "We're free now! Everything's going to be okay!" I assured her, yes, we're all free and things were wonderful. I helped get her back to bed; she was cold so I got out another blanket and turned down the air conditioner. I was cold, too. Mom went back to sleep after singing a strange version of 'Silent Night'. Her sleep talking made me miss my grandbaby; I'd only seen him in short visits. I prayed, knowing my time with him would come later. For now, I had to stay in this season of life.

September 2

"Fear not, for I am with you; be not dismayed, for I am your God;"
Isaiah 41:10

Mom fell again. She was coloring in the dining room when I heard her say she wanted to go outside. I ran from the kitchen to stop her in time to see her stumble between the chairs, and down she went. Praying, I called emergency Lift and Assist and soon a fire truck with four large firemen arrived. Mom had a bloody hand and elbow and a big bruise on her left hip, but otherwise seemed fine. As the firefighters were helping get her off the floor she yelled out in pain; she said it hurt where they were lifting her. But she showed them she could walk and even did a little dance. She asked if any of them were her students and was sad when they left. All seemed fine. Key word, "seemed" …

September 3

"In the day of my trouble I call upon you, for you answer me." **Psalm 86:7**

Around midnight after Mom's fall she called for me saying she was in pain. I checked her vitals and she asked, very seriously, "Do you remember when you were little we went to the courthouse where we saw that planet almost drop from the sky? There was so much light, and Jesus came down and brought a bunch of people with Him." I said I didn't remember, trying not to look too incredulous. "You were very little, but I'm not making it up, it really did happen." I put her on oxygen; she soon fell asleep. At 4:30 a.m. she yelled out again saying her shoulder and arm hurt. I gave her pain meds and called hospice; they ordered an x-ray. I prayed for healing, holding Mom's hand as she cried…

September 4

"The light of the eyes rejoices the heart, and good news refreshes the bones."
Proverbs 15:30

The x-ray tech didn't get to the house until after 10 a.m. The x-rays showed that Mom had fractured her 2nd right rib, probably from bumping into the chair when she fell. It also explained why she yelled out in pain when the fireman lifted her. Nurse Leslie told me there was nothing that could be done about a cracked rib other than bedrest and pain management. The good news was that the x-rays showed that the pneumonia was clearing up. After Leslie left, Mom sat in her chair singing happily and asked if she could take a walk outside...She always called herself 'Tough Huff' (her maiden name) and yes, she was very tough. Praise God.

September 5

"Look at the birds of the air: they neither sow nor reap nor gather into barns, and yet your heavenly Father feeds them. Are you not of more value than they?" **Matthew 6:26**

It was an especially exhausting day. As we say in East Texas, "Mom wore me ragged". After lunch she swore she hadn't eaten, so I gave her the same meal again and she ate every bite. She wanted up, down, outside, inside, food, cookies, colder water, just everything/anything she could think of. I was also busy re-dressing the wounds from her fall and giving her additional pain patches and medications, so I wasn't able to rest all day and night. The entire time I prayed for God to help both of us. I needed Mom to heal fast so my own MS symptoms would stay at bay. I also prayed for extra grace, because as my strength diminished, so did my patience.

September 6

"For I will satisfy the weary soul, and every languishing soul I will replenish." **Matthew 11:28-30**

Mom had now been on hospice 5 months so she had to be recertified. A nurse came over and after checking Mom's vitals told me she would remain certified "as long as needed". She was concerned about Mom's left knee, still very swollen after her fall. We talked about getting it x-rayed but at this point surgery wasn't an option anyway. But the nurse said she was also worried about me after noticing that I was dragging my foot when I walked, something that happens when MS is flaring. "You look weary," she said. All correct, but I reminded her there was nothing I could do about it other than pray. As long as I was able to stay upright, I had to keep going--and only with God's help.

September 7

"For the anger of man does not produce the righteousness of God." **James 1:20**

It seemed like a wonderful day for Mom and me. In spite of my MS pain, I took her on several walk and rolls, and after helping with her shower I gave her a facial and even put some makeup on her. It was above and beyond our usual day. But when Lisa came home I heard her complaining that I was "always mad at her". It hurt my feelings but it also made me recognize that I definitely wasn't smiling much all day and a few times I was less patient than usual because of the pain. I prayed for God to help me remain kind and compassionate towards her. On days like this it was hard to forgive myself, but I was grateful that Jesus always would.

September 8

"Only take care, and keep your soul diligently, lest you forget the things that your eyes have seen, and lest they depart from your heart all the days of your life. Make them known to your children and your children's children—" **Deuteronomy 4:9**

And after the darkness, such light! Jason and Mimi brought the baby to the house. He slept the entire time but Mom was overjoyed to finally see her great-grandson. While she was admittedly never very good with babies and little children, she was completely in her element with high school students. "I've just never liked children, not even my own," she often joked to anyone listening. And yet on this day, her heart seemed to change when she held her great-grandson. I thanked God for bringing that little boy into our world before Mom had to leave it.

September 9

"For everything there is a season, and a time for every matter under heaven: a time to be born, and a time to die; a time to plant, and a time to pluck up what is planted;" **Ecclesiastes 3:1-2**

Another season was approaching. I changed the living room decor with Fall colors, golden yellows and oranges and pale greens. Pumpkins and our trusty scarecrows were placed on the front porch. By now I'd become used to Mom's terrible breathing and it didn't scare me anymore; as long as she was comfortable and happy, I was fine, too. We were both only sleeping a few hours at night doing breathing treatments and replacing her oxygen tube when she got up looking for cookies. The storms were approaching, but for now I was grateful to God for the calm.

September 10

"For my father and my mother have forsaken me, but the Lord will take me in." **Psalm 27:10**

It was a long day with nurse visits, cleaning house, making dinner and thinking we had a wonderful day together. When Lisa came home I went to my room to rest while they watched an episode of "Little House". When Lisa putting Mom to bed I heard her from the monitor telling Lisa, "You're the only one who ever takes care of me." My heart broke a little so I prayed for the Holy Spirit to help me keep things in perspective. Lisa, knowing the monitor was on, texted me as soon as she got to her room: "We know the truth; we know what's real. I love you." I didn't want it to hurt, but I prayed for the pain to stop, both physical and emotional...

September 11

"For from his fullness we have all received, grace upon grace." **John 1:16**

I'd finally fallen asleep after midnight when I heard someone in my room calling my name. It was only Mom but it scared me to death. She said her bed had "deflated" so I took her back to her room. The bed was fine except the sheets were bunched up at the bottom. I fixed them and helped her back in. In her bathroom I noticed she'd cleaning her hairbrush in the sink again, which was now clogged. I'd deal with that later. She was wheezing more than usual and said she was 'hurting all over'. I put her on oxygen and gave her pain meds. "Thank you for taking such good care of me all the time," she said. She took my hand and held it to her face, smiling up at me. (Thank you for that, Lord. I needed that.)

September 12

"The grass withers, the flower fades when the breath of the Lord blows on it; surely the people are grass." **Isaiah 40:7**

Mom's lungs were getting worse. She now needed breathing treatments every 4 hours and was on oxygen almost the entire day and night, with pain meds and anything else possible to keep her comfortable and safe. Meanwhile I was becoming weaker, too, with almost no sleep and allowing stress to take over too often. I needed God to hold me up because it was starting to feel like Mom was needing more than I could give.

September 13

"For this light momentary affliction is preparing for us an eternal weight of glory beyond all comparison," 2 **Corinthians 4:17**

Little things were becoming problems for Mom now. Walking short distances, even from the bathroom back to her chair, left her breathless and wheezing. One morning just after having a breathing treatment we walked to the patio and she could barely breathe. At this point there was nothing else we could do but pray; Mom's right lung was losing more air capacity every day. Life was changing again, as were the leaves on the Japanese maple in our front yard...

September 14

"Heal the sick who are there and tell them, 'The kingdom of God has come near to you.'" **Luke 10:9 (NIV)**

Mom was struggling to breathe as usual, but now she was saying her chest and back were burning. She sounded incredibly rattly so I was certain she had pneumonia again. A hospice nurse visited and said both of Mom's lungs sounded "horrible" with very little capacity. We decided there wasn't a need for another x-ray machine, we could both hear the pneumonia from a standing position. She ordered antibiotics and I called Lisa to let her know. And then I went to my room and prayed for strength and courage before beginning my vigil at Mom's bedside.

September 15

"Do not forsake your friend or a friend of your family, and do not go to your relative's house when disaster strikes you—better a neighbor nearby than a relative far away." **Proverbs 27:10**

Lisa cared for Mom so my friend Amy Nelson could drive me to my MS infusion. The pre-med drugs always knocked me out so I was able to sleep (albeit drug-induced) for the first time in many months. Amy picked me up when I was finished, almost 4 hours later. We had a nice lunch and then she stayed and talked to Mom while I went to bed. I thank God for such a wonderful friend, there for me through the highs and lows of life, ready to help at almost any moment, even with burdens of their own. I prayed then, and now, to be as good a friend as my friends have been to me.

September 16

"The Lord sustains him on his sickbed; in his illness you restore him to full health." **Psalm 41:3**

Mom was awake around 9:30 a.m. Out of habit, I got up to fix breakfast and give her medications. As soon as I finished I realized I needed to lie back down; the first few days after my infusion were always difficult for me. I straightened up the living room, then texted Lisa to please take over for me. I went back to bed, recognizing that if. I didn't take care of myself and remember to *"be still and know that I am God"* I'd never be able to help my mother. This time, I didn't have a choice. I had to stop and allow God to heal me.

September 17

"Let us therefore strive to enter that rest, so that no one may fall by the same sort of disobedience." **Hebrews 4:11**

The steroids from my infusion were hitting me hard. I was restless and felt strange all night and morning, unable to sleep. At 5 a.m. I helped Mom when she couldn't find her extra diapers, and then at 7:30 a.m. I heard her saying "What's the word? I can't remember the word!" It sounded like she was struggling with a seek and find puzzle in her dreams. I was up for the day so I made her breakfast and realized I needed help again. My "energy" was artificial and if I didn't rest I'd collapse. I went to my room after Lisa took over, but instead of resting I switched out my entire closet from summer to fall. Exhausted, I had to pray again for the ability to BE STILL. Soon after I finally slept a few hours.

September 18

"For you know that the testing of your faith produces steadfastness."
James 1:3

I still wasn't feeling great but tried to keep Mom busy all day. We went outside where I dug up dead tomato vines and propped up the last surviving bell pepper plant. I went inside to quickly wash my hands, leaving Mom in a chair on the patio. When I got back she was hobbling in the yard without her walker, picking up a very large rock. She grinned and waved at me, proudly showing me her rock. I ran to help her back, praying thanks to God that she didn't fall. By lunch we were both worn out. Mom still had pneumonia and was still wheezing and struggling, and I was in still in pain. We were both a mess, but happy. Praise God.

September 19

"For as we share abundantly in Christ's sufferings, so through Christ we share abundantly in comfort too." **2 Corinthians 1:5**

Another difficult night with my poor mother. I barely slept, listening to her rough breathing on the monitor. It was heartbreaking. Around 3 a.m. I heard her in the bathroom; all the lights were on. I helped her back to bed and put her on oxygen. She was crying. "How long do I have to go on like this?" she asked. I knew she meant her suffering but I smiled and said, "Everyone has to pee at night mom!" She chuckled. I wanted her to feel "normal" again. I turned off her bedside light while stroking her hair. Back in my room I heard her fall asleep but I stayed up praying. My day had begun.

September 20

"But I will sing of your strength; I will sing aloud of your steadfast love in the morning. For you have been to me a fortress and a refuge in the day of my distress." **Psalm 59:16**

Mom was confused about where (and who) she was so I put her on oxygen and called hospice. Despite all the new strong medications her lungs were worse. Feeling helpless, I took her on a walk and roll. Very hoarsely, she sang her unusual new mixture of the songs 'Everything is Beautiful' and 'Have Thine Own Way, Lord'. It went like this: "Everything is beautiful in its own way, I am the potter, thou art the clay" (and yes, she got that part wrong, too). She was happy and wanted to sit in the front yard and sing awhile longer. She said it was the best part of her entire day; mine, too.

September 21

"I sought the Lord, and he answered me and delivered me from all my fears." **Psalm 34:4**

This day marked two beginnings: Sundowning, and the saga of 'the very bad man'. Mom was convinced that a bad guy was in the neighborhood and on his way to our house. She became obsessed with finding her daddy's shotgun, always adding, "I know how to use it, and I will, too." Mom also had high fever; I was sure that either the pneumonia was back or it never left. Nurse Heather came over and helped calm her for a little while, but Mom never stopped believing there was a bad guy either inside or outside the house, day and night. I began a prayer that would continue to the very end—that Mom would find peace.

September 22

"Therefore, preparing your minds for action, and being sober-minded, set your hope fully on the grace that will be brought to you at the revelation of Jesus Christ." **1 Peter 1:13**

Mom's pneumonia was worse. She was hurting so I helped her into an almost hot shower and put pain patches on her back. Then she started talking about the bad guy again, demanding her gun. Lisa and I tried telling her he was already in jail but she didn't believe us. She was becoming frantic and angry to the point that I called hospice. They told me to give her .05 morphine for pain and to help with her delusions. I cried as I filled the vial but then I heard Mom searching for her gun in her closet, muttering about wanting to "kill that man". I prayed as I gave her the medicine, much more confident in what I needed to do to help her.

September 23

"For this is a gracious thing, when, mindful of God, one endures sorrows while suffering unjustly." **1 Peter 2:19**

With everything Mom forgot, including her 53-year marriage to Dad, it was shocking how long she held on to the 'very bad man'. One strange moment occurred when Mom was in her chair listening to gospel music. She got up, did a crazy little dance, and told me she wanted her gun. Laughing almost maniacally, she took off almost running towards her bedroom to search. Other times she'd tell me she needed to use the restroom but then I'd find her searching in her closet again or digging in a dresser drawer, searching, searching. My prayers were becoming desperate pleas for help.

September 24

"Behold! I tell you a mystery. We shall not all sleep, but we shall all be changed," **1 Corinthians 15:51**

In the midst of everything, my Virginia friend John Baldwin died. I didn't know he was so sick, especially because he consistently texted prayers for us, never mentioning anything about his own ailments. He sent us audio prayers and songs and mailed us cd's he created with his favorite music. John was planning to visit us in Texas; he'd never been here and wanted to see a Dallas Cowboy's game. I was later told he didn't want to "burden" me about his pending death because he knew how much I was already going through. It broke my heart that I couldn't pray for my friend the way he prayed for us. Praise God for friends like John, who teach us how to become better people.

September 25

"Blessed are the pure in heart, for they shall see God." **Matthew 5:8 (NIV)**

When I was packing up Mom and Dad's underground house I found a box of sermons that my (biological) father Jerry Bledsoe wrote. On sleepless nights I'd read them, in awe of his beautiful writing. His sermons were very forward-thinking for the late 1950's and early 1960's, including social topics like race relations. There were also various notes about being unafraid of death and the importance of being ready whenever your time comes. His notes were incredibly prophetic, considering he died in a car wreck at age 33. I was already honored to be his daughter, and even more after reading the way he honored Jesus.

September 26

"Humble yourselves, therefore, under God's mighty hand, that he may lift you up in due time." **I Peter 5:6**

Sundowning was in full force even before breakfast, and as usual Mom was becoming frantic about guns and bad guys. I could usually talk her down, but on this day she became so paranoid that I ended up yelling at her. I had to stop myself, pray, and went outside to call Lisa to come home. I'd only been out a few moments but found Mom in my room, searching for her gun. When Lisa got home she saw how upset I was. It wasn't just Mom; it was the death of Dad, and Tina and now John. I was also concerned that Mom might become out of control like Dad. It was all too much so I had to give it to Jesus, the only One who could handle it. Because that day, I certainly couldn't.

September 27

"O God, from my youth you have taught me, and I still proclaim your wondrous deeds. So even to old age and gray hairs, O God, do not forsake me, until I proclaim your might to another generation, your power to all those to come." **Psalm 71:17-18**

Early morning I heard Mom wandering in the hall. Thankfully all she wanted this time was a cookie so I took her to the kitchen. It was almost 1 a.m. but she was wide awake, happily eating her cookie. We were in the midst of full-on sundowning and Mom was in the 'terrible twos' phase, sort of an adult toddler. Just like Dad once did, she rarely slept, banging around in her room all night until the sun came up. My morning routine now was to get up around 5 or 6 a.m., pray over my coffee, and try to steady myself for the day.

September 28

"Then our mouth was filled with laughter, and our tongue with shouts of joy; then they said among the nations, "The Lord has done great things for them." **Psalm 126:2**

Mom was always hungry after her breathing treatments so we tried moving dinner to 4 p.m. instead of 5. This didn't work because at 5 she'd ask for supper again. One night while eating meal #2 Mom looked at her plate and said, "Last night one of my kinfolk tried to poison me." I told her Lisa and I were the only kinfolk in the house. She looked at us, raised her right eyebrow high (the way she did as a schoolteacher) and shrugged. We burst out laughing as she remained straight-faced. I thanked God for moments like that; they got us through the bad ones.

September 29

"How many are your works, Lord! In wisdom you made them all; the earth is full of your creatures." **Psalm 104:24**

In addition to collecting rocks, books, cookie jars, and spoons from every state, in Mom's Alzheimer's years she also started collecting elephants. One day she started talking about how special they were, calling them the most 'beautiful creature God ever made' and somewhere in her mind she felt it was her responsibility to gather as many as she could. Almost everywhere we went she'd find a new elephant to add to her collection; some ceramic or metal, others were stuffed. And once some of her "Mrs. Brown" fans learned about her latest craze they started giving her elephants either personally or in the mail. By then Lisa and I wanted her to be as happy as possible. And praise the Lord, elephants were a big help.

September 30

"Bear one another's burdens, and so fulfill the law of Christ." **Galatians 6:2**

It was a rough one. Taken verbatim from the 2022 note in my journal: "Feeling powerless with Mom. She's suffering, struggling. I'm up with her all hours of the night and early morning and I'm just so tired. Keeping my eyes, mind, and heart on God. I know He is here giving me rest when I need it. But yes, this is hard and only getting harder. Without Him I can't imagine how anyone could survive this. She has bronchitis and all new meds, but I'm not afraid. I can't be."

October

"The grass withers, the flower fades, but the word of our God will stand forever."
Isaiah 40:8

October 1

"See that you do not despise one of these little ones. For I tell you that in heaven their angels always see the face of my Father who is in heaven."
Matthew 18:10

Lisa's son, Zack, came to visit from Dallas. This would be the last time he would see his grandmother, and the first to see his new baby cousin. Jason and Zack were always close, only two months apart in age and they spent a good portion of their childhood together in California. I was blessed that while everyone visited, I got to spend time alone with my grandson, just holding and rocking him. After eating, Mom came in the room to see him, too, and I let her hold him for just a moment. Tears streamed down her face as she stared at her great-grandchild, asleep in her arms. Did she know this would be her last time, too?

October 2

"He who dwells in the shelter of the Most High will abide in the shadow of the Almighty." **Psalm 91:1**

"Full-on crazy" was the only way to describe Mom when Nurse Heather came to check on her. The 'very bad man' was back in her head and, as usual lately, she was mad at Lisa and me because we wouldn't give her a gun. Heather was wonderful; she knelt by Mom's chair and told her Jesus wouldn't want her to be a murderer. "That man is in your head, Mrs. Brown, and the only way to 'kill' him is through medicine." That day Heather instructed me to give Mom sundowner meds from the refrigerator to help keep her calm. I prayed for patience like never before and would need even more very soon.

October 3

"Let my cry come before you, O Lord; give me understanding according to your word!" **Psalm 119:169**

I could no longer leave Mom alone at all. Much like a toddler, if I left the room for even a few moments she would do something that could potentially hurt her. After she moved her crossword puzzle table across the room for no reason, I had a tiny breakdown by myself in the kitchen. I was weary, becoming physically and emotionally broken. I prayed for emergency help and instantly felt better. When Lisa got home, even though she didn't like doing puzzles she sat with Mom so I could start dinner. Later that night Mom told Lisa, "Some woman was here trying to do my puzzle!" She forgot it was Lisa and felt bad when I told her. Our poor mother was so mixed up.

October 4

"I have said these things to you, that in me you may have peace. In the world you will have tribulation. But take heart; I have overcome the world."
John 16:33

It was a day of accusations. Mom accused me of stealing the book that she was holding in her hands. When I pointed out the book, she said I must have put it in her hands after taking it away. She later said I made her stop working on her puzzle after telling me she didn't want to do it anymore. Then she accused me of coloring in her book. After taking a moment to pray and breathe, I suggested we sit on the patio. I asked her if she remembered Dad when he was sundowning, hoping it would trigger a memory. "He got a little crazy," she said, then excitedly pointed at a squirrel. She was happy again, for a moment. I thanked God for His squirrels...

October 5

"The Lord is near to the brokenhearted and saves the crushed in spirit."
Psalm 34:18

I had to get my bi-annual MRI's at the hospital so Lisa stayed with Mom. When I got home Lisa was crying and Mom was furiously cracking nuts at the dining table, "busy work" that Lisa thought might keep her calm. She said Mom had been throwing a tantrum, banging the nutcracker on the table. When Lisa tried to take it away Mom hit her with it; there was a large bruise on Lisa's hand. Mom never looked up as I told her I'd been in the hospital, thinking it might shake her up. She coldly looked at me and said, "I don't feel so great myself" and continued cracking nuts. "Get the pills," I told Lisa. We sat with her as the storm passed, knowing how blessed she was to have us, even when she forgot.

October 6

"Therefore, my dear brothers and sisters, stand firm. Let nothing move you. Always give yourselves fully to the work of the Lord, because you know that your labor in the Lord is not in vain." **I Corinthians 15:58 (NIV)**

This stage of Mom's Alzheimer's was very frustrating and sad for all of us. In the same way she had forgot Dad or how to read and write, she was now forgetting the "adult" way to express her frustrations. Her confusion showed up in rages, tantrums, and defiance. I had to react more like a mother than a daughter. And since I wasn't able to sleep at night I spent much more time in scripture and writing. Caregiving was becoming a test of wills, but God managed to keep me almost supernaturally strong, patient, and kind.

October 7

"And now these three remain: faith, hope and love. But the greatest of these is love." **1 Corinthians 13:13**

The sundowner meds were finally helping. The "bad man" was still alive in her head, but not as constant. On this day after her shower and shampoo Mom was in her bedroom rocking chair, happily singing from her Methodist hymnal. She thanked me many times, telling me how clean and fresh she felt. I sat next to her and told her I loved her. And in this clear, calm moment, I told her, "Mom, in an hour things might change and you'll feel angry again. But I always know you love me, okay?" She seemed to understand and said she didn't know why she got that way. For a lovely moment, I was talking to my mama. Praise Jesus: I know He was there with us.

October 8

"I will not give sleep to my eyes or slumber to my eyelids," **Psalm 132:4**

Mom had a great day coloring and working on her puzzle with very little anger or frustration. But around midnight, it started again. She got up multiple times, first looking in her closet for her gun, and later looking for a book. I helped her back to bed and gave her oxygen because she was wheezing from her activities. An hour later I heard her again, this time dragging the very heavy oxygen machine down the hall. She finally settled down around 2 a.m. and just as I started to fall asleep she was out of bed again: She wanted a cookie. I got her two, took her to the bathroom, then back to bed. She finally fell asleep, but I never did. I prayed until the sun came up for God to keep me steady for whatever was next.

October 9

"For you shall go out in joy and be led forth in peace; the mountains and the hills before you shall break forth into singing, and all the trees of the field shall clap their hands." **Isaiah 55:12**

Jason and Mimi needed help so I spent the day cleaning and organizing their house, making it more efficient for their busy lifestyles. It was also wonderful to be with my baby grandson awhile. During lunch Jason told me he'd been thinking about my biological father, Jerry. We talked about how short his life was and what a wonderful grandfather he would have been. I shared some of my favorite memories, recalling how joyfully he lived. The blessing is that while everyone eventually loses their earthly fathers, we have the best Father of all, the One who never leaves us.

October 10

"I will instruct you and teach you in the way you should go; I will counsel you with my eye upon you." **Psalm 31:3**

Mom was finally sleeping soundly so I started my evening prayers. Out of nowhere, I began crying so hard my cat Dagny jumped on the bed to comfort me. I went to Lisa's room and talked to her about how hard it was medicating Mom to calm her, even though I understood the reasons why. The meds helped quell her fears about 'the bad man' and calmed the rage it took for her to hit Lisa. As always, our talk ended in laughter. Back in my room, I said prayers of gratitude that I had my sister with me. I also prayed about Dad and our Grandma Birdie Lee, both who died of Alzheimer's. I knew the ending wouldn't be easy for any of us, but with God holding our hands, we'd be just fine...

October 11

"And call upon me in the day of trouble; I will deliver you, and you shall glorify me." **Psalm 50:15**

My health was declining. Over the years I was able to manage Multiple Sclerosis as long as everything was in balance with food, sleep, and minimal stress. Now, with all those things out the window, even a healthy person would have issues. Even more than usual, I was stumbling, dropping things, and the pain at night was much worse. It was difficult to talk to my neurologist on the phone because Mom got paranoid when she wasn't involved with the call. ("Why aren't they talking to me? Is that my doctor? Why can't I talk, too?") Respite wasn't an option for many reasons, so I turned to prayer and the blind faith that Jesus would get me through everything I needed to do. And He did.

October 12

"Let your gentleness be evident to all. The Lord is near." **Philippians 4:5 (NIV)**

Mom slept much more than usual, probably due to new meds. One night after dinner she went to the bathroom and then got in bed by herself, something she never did, not even when she had pneumonia. I put her new walker nearby; her cane wasn't sturdy enough anymore. An hour or so later I heard her searching through her bedside drawers; but this time she was looking for three little stuffed animals she'd been carrying around the past week. They were in the living room so I brought them to her, and she tucked them under the sheets with her. She slept all night and I said extra prayers because my mother's life was once again changing.

October 13

"And the Lord answered me: "Write the vision; make it plain on tablets, so he may run who reads it." **Habakkuk 2:2**

I couldn't sleep so I read my Bible until I drifted off and had one of my frequent 'flying dreams'. It started with a voice telling me, "You can still fly, just run and let go." In my dream I flew higher than ever before, beyond the skies, the planets, until I was in complete darkness. Then I entered into an extraordinary all-encompassing light that seemed to surround me, or maybe I absorbed into it. I sensed family around me and people I didn't know. It wasn't warm or cold, it was something more. And then I was back, hearing Mom coughing, struggling. But I was at peace, better. Grateful. Ready to face whatever came next.

October 14

"A hot-tempered man stirs up strife, but he who is slow to anger quiets contention." **Proverbs 15:18**

Mom was up around 9 a.m. in a feisty mood. I did all I could to keep her happy, coloring with her, taking her on a walk and roll, but nothing worked. After lunch, for the first time in years, she said she wanted to watch the news. I told her I didn't know how to turn on the living room television and that was the truth; for some reason, it took 3 remotes to turn on that tv so Lisa always handled it. Mom didn't believe me and angrily said, "Give them to me!" I handed her the remotes and went to the kitchen to pray for patience. To my surprise, she somehow managed to find the YouTube channel so I listened as my mother watched beauty instructor, Tati, teaching her how to apply blush...

October 15

"Thus says the Lord: "Stand by the roads, and look, and ask for the ancient paths, where the good way is; and walk in it, and find rest for your souls." **Jeremiah 6:16**

Despite knowing how difficult it was to leave Mom, I needed time with my 'wise counsel' friends Julia and Kristen. We met for lunch and they brought me a gift bag full of Christian nursery books for the grandbaby, and coffee from Oklahoma. I cried as we prayed together. God certainly knew I needed them because when I got home Mom was on the floor. Moments before, she had fallen almost on top of Lisa. The firemen came and all was fine, but Lisa was shaken up. Thanks to time spent with my friends I was able to remain calm and helped both of them with much more grace and patience. Praise God.

October 16

"But you, O Lord, do not be far off! O you my help, come quickly to my aid!" **Psalm 22:19**

The three of us were watching a movie when I looked over and noticed Mom was choking. I flung off everything that was in my lap—reading glasses, my phone—and ran over to help her at the same time as Lisa, who also heard her gagging. We sat her forward and she coughed up a soft peppermint. After saying a very loud prayer of gratitude, I thought of all the ways we were already closely watching her. Now, as I took away her beloved candy dish forever, this included the way she ate food...

October 17

"Prepare your work outside; get everything ready for yourself in the field, and after that build your house." **Proverbs 24:27**

I've always been a 'nester'. As a child in South Texas, during hurricane season I would put all my dolls and stuffed animals in pillowcases, preparing for disaster. When moving or traveling, I packed early and unpacked immediately. Now, it was time to reevaluate Mom's bedroom again, planning for the next coming phase. When I finished, her room was still home-y and comfortable but more practical. The bed was now against the wall so she couldn't fall out and the floor was open for her wheelchair, which she used much more now. I believe my nesting and organizing skills were a gift from God, certainly useful while caregiving.

October 18

"The Lord will fight for you, and you have only to be silent." **Exodus 14:14**

Another season was arriving; the weather was getting cooler now and life for all of us a little more difficult. Mom's sleep pattern was completely upside-down; she was up all night so she often slept until noon. Despite all the powerful meds and breathing treatments, nothing helped her cough or rough breathing anymore. I was also now changing her diaper when she wasn't able to get to the bathroom in time. But the biggest and saddest change was that Mom was losing her words and didn't talk much now. So other than a constant dialogue with God in my head, I wasn't talking much either. Life was becoming deafeningly silent.

October 19

"Therefore I tell you, whatever you ask in prayer, believe that you have received it, and it will be yours." **Mark 11:24**

I needed someone to help bathe Mom now, so hospice sent over a worker who did everything except blow-dry her hair, something I loved doing myself. Lisa also started coming home early on Wednesdays, a much-needed break for me. But during my down time I still had to take care of housecleaning and maintenance, which is what I did on this day. While Lisa and Mom watched a movie, I mopped, vacuumed, and dusted, then cleaned and scrubbed the bathrooms. When finished, I noticed tingling in my legs and arms, very bad MS signs. I needed to rest. This time in addition to my usual prayers, I prayed for my own healing. I couldn't help my mother if I collapsed, too…

October 20

"Fear not, little flock, for it is your Father's good pleasure to give you the kingdom." **Luke 12:32**

I rolled Mom into the kitchen so she could sit in her wheelchair with me while I cooked dinner. Then, for the first time, she discovered that she could wheel the chair by herself. For almost 30 minutes she wheeled around the hallway, the living room, and to the front door to watch squirrels. She was so proud of herself and it was also the most exercise she'd had in over a year. Best of all, after months of eating dinner in her living room chair, she wheeled her chair to the dining table. I didn't know how long this would last, but the three of us were once again eating a meal together, praise God.

October 21

"Peace I leave with you; my peace I give to you. Not as the world gives do I give to you. Let not your hearts be troubled, neither let them be afraid."
John 14:27

Lisa was having a very stressful time at work. In the past it helped when she was able to take Mom to the nearby pond to feed the ducks, or talking and laughing during dinner together.. But other than the night before, Mom was eating meals in her living room chair again, insisting she couldn't move. So Lisa and Mom mostly watched 'Little House' episodes together, and she took over the bedtime routine for me.. At this point, we both had to push our personal problems aside and cherish whatever time we had left with our mother.

October 22

"Make your father and mother happy; give your mother a reason to be glad." **Proverbs 23:25 (NCV)**

Mom was having trouble adjusting to our new nighttime schedule. Lisa and I had very different styles of caregiving; I was the "strict parent" all week while Lisa was more like the "fun aunt". I never watched television during the day; Mom and I went on wheelchair walks (when the weather was nice), worked on puzzles or colored. Lisa preferred watching movies and old television classics. It was also an adjustment for Mom when I left her with Lisa after years of being her mostly sole caregiver. Her diseases were making her even more restless, frustrated, and angry, so I prayed constantly, unceasingly, trying to find balance in all our lives.

October 23

"Good sense makes one slow to anger, and it is his glory to overlook an offense." **Proverbs 19:11**

At 2 a.m. I heard Mom yelling for help. I ran, expecting to find her on the floor but instead found her, upright, in the bathroom. She was furious, insisting that someone had been going through her drawers. She demanded to know what happened to "all her stuff". Relieved she wasn't hurt, I prayed for patience and realized she was disoriented because I'd recently cleaned and reorganized her bathroom. She was looking for her diapers, previously stored in the drawer but they were now on top of the counter where I thought she would find them easier. After I explained and apologized she settled down and I got her to bed, but she was still very angry, grinding her teeth. Forever more, no more changes.

October 24

"But you do not know what will happen tomorrow! Your life is like a mist. You can see it for a short time, but then it goes away." **James 4:14 (NCV)**

I couldn't go back to sleep the night before so I watched television and read my Bible and devotionals until the sun came up. I'd just finished when I heard Mom calling, "Ann-Marie, anybody, come help me!" As usual, I ran to her room, but this time she was sitting up, smiling and looking happy. I felt breath pouring out of me, in a good way. I wheeled her in front of the French doors so she could watch the early birds and squirrels while I made breakfast. I offered God mighty prayers that morning, listening to my mother singing a broken version of 'How Great Thou Art'. Yes, He is.

October 25

"But God, being rich in mercy, because of the great love with which he loved us," **Ephesians 2:4**

For the 4th time Mom fell again, this time from a sitting position. I was right there, but because of MS issues I wasn't strong enough to help. She screamed all the way down, ending up face-down on the floor. Other than her glasses nothing was broken, no blood. While on the phone with 911 Lift and Assist, Mom yelled out, "Is anyone coming to take me away? I want to die!" I prayed aloud for Jesus to help her pain and confusion. The fire department arrived almost immediately, easily lifting Mom into her chair. I thought of all the traumas she'd been through the past few months: pneumonia twice, 4 falls, a broken rib. Was I a terrible caregiver? I prayed again, this time for mercy…

October 26

"They won't be afraid of bad news, their hearts are steady because they trust the Lord." **Psalm 112:7 (NCV)**

Mom was eating much less lunch now, something hospice told us to watch out for. She was coughing and wheezing more than usual and despite breathing treatments in the middle of the night and early mornings, nothing was helping. She was now always coughing so hard she'd grasp her chest, crying. It was always burning now, and after a bad coughing fit she would often fall asleep from sheer exhaustion. At night she didn't want us to close her door anymore so I'd stay and sing gospel songs to her or say the Lord's Prayer with her. And later I'd say prayers for myself, to keep all fear at bay and to trust His will, always.

October 27

"Not domineering over those in your charge, but being examples to the flock." **I Peter 5:3**

Early morning I heard Mom talking loudly in her room so I went to check on her. She looked at me and angrily said, "I saw him and her together." Out of curiosity I asked who she was talking about. "You know who. Him. And her. They were together in the lunchroom." I asked again who "they" were and she now looked at me skeptically and said, "It could've been you, or not you, with him." I started to sit down on the bed to rationalize and pray with her but she said I was hurting her leg. I wasn't anywhere near her leg; she was just angry. I kissed her on the cheek, told her I loved her and left. It was obviously a bad dream, one I hoped she'd forget along with everything else.

October 28

"Honor your father and your mother, that your days may be long in the land that the Lord your God is giving you." **Exodus 20:12**

I sometimes posted caregiving stories on social media, sharing the uplifting moments as well as difficult ones. Responses were mostly positive but sometimes I'd hear from people who thought I'd taken on too much, suggesting Mom might be better off in a nursing home with "professional" care. To be honest, when she struggled to breathe or fell down I sometimes had those thoughts, too. But both parents had "professional" care that resulted in tragedy. Whatever happened to Mom would be under the careful scrutiny of Lisa and me, our caring hospice team, and mostly our loving God who was guiding every moment.

October 29

"So, whether you eat or drink, or whatever you do, do all to the glory of God." **1 Corinthians 10:31**

When I went to Mom's room to help her to breakfast she was already sitting up with her "babies", the 3 little stuffed animals. Smiling, she told me she had a dream about food and was "very hungry". I made her a big breakfast with bacon, scrambled eggs and toast and for the first time in weeks she ate almost all of it. I ate with her, too, usually opting only for coffee in the mornings. After breakfast she fell fast asleep in her chair while we were coloring. I prayed thanks for such a nice morning and for the little moments of calm before the bridges broke…

October 30

"God is not unjust; he will not forget your work and the love you have shown him as you have helped his people and continue to help them."
Hebrews 6:10 (NIV)

Our beloved nurse Heather was leaving the hospice company. From the beginning she had been such a force in our world, helping and teaching all of us through everything. I couldn't imagine caregiving without her and I even considered changing companies, but I didn't want to lose Nurse Leslie, too. Heather would return to our family later in major ways, but for now we had to say goodbye to a wonderful friend. Some nurses aren't gifted by God; maybe they choose nursing as a profession instead of a calling. Heather was a naturally gifted nurse and what a blessing she was to our family (and still is).

October 31

"My flesh and my heart may fail, but God is the strength of my heart and my portion forever." **Psalm 73:26**

It was laundry day for both Mom and me. I washed and changed all our bedding, bathroom rugs, and everything else washable. To keep her busy, Mom helped me fold the clothes while I put the sheets on our beds. After that we went on a walk and roll and then she wanted me to color with her. As I was setting up everything I suddenly felt exhausted. My MS issues were at an all-time high and I'd hit the proverbial wall. I told Mom I needed to rest so she needed to color by herself awhile. She got mad; like a child she had no concept of anyone else's cares. All I could do was pray harder as I lay on the couch watching her color, gritting her teeth and angry…

November

"The Lord is my strength and my shield; in him my heart trusts, and I am helped; my heart exults, and with my song I give thanks to him."
Psalm 28:7

November 1

"And it shall come to pass afterward, that I will pour out my Spirit on all flesh; your sons and your daughters shall prophesy, your old men shall dream dreams, and your young men shall see visions." **Joel 2:28**

"The man said we have to go home now," Mom told me. It was the first of several times to come that "people" were telling her it was time for her to 'go home'. At 4 a.m. she was sitting on the edge of her bed holding an empty Kleenex box that now housed her 3 little stuffed animals. She'd been awake all night calling out to me, and every time I got her back to bed she'd call me again, insisting she was leaving soon. She finally slept around 9 a.m. after I explained that she needed to rest for her trip. Then I prayed for supernatural strength; it was November and I would need it.

November 2

"Or do you not know that your body is a temple of the Holy Spirit within you, whom you have from God? You are not your own, for you were bought with a price. So glorify God in your body." **1 Corinthians 6:19-20**

I helped Mom to the bathroom and after a time she yelled out, "Ann-Marie, come look!" I ran, never knowing what I might find, and saw something amazing. Barely able to walk anymore, Mom had somehow managed to move the shower chair out of the shower. She had placed it in front of the mirror where she was proudly sitting and brushing her hair, something she hadn't done by herself in months. Considering her fall record it was incredible that she was now moving furniture and grooming herself. Something was definitely changing inside her, praise God, but it also felt like she was preparing to leave us soon...

November 3

"Do not repay evil for evil or reviling for reviling, but on the contrary, bless, for to this you were called, that you may obtain a blessing." **I Peter 3:9**

Mom and I shared a beautiful moment the previous night when she asked me to read aloud from her Bible. But the next morning when it wasn't on her nightstand she accused me of stealing it. I brought it from the living room and as I handed it to her she asked why I took it in the first place. I reminded her we were reading scripture the night before but she was mad and didn't believe me. Nothing I said helped so I started to leave. "Can I stay in my room and sit by the window the rest of my life or will you take that away from me, too?" she asked. I went over and hugged her, then went to my room and prayed on my knees for patience and kindness. All before breakfast…

November 4

"When the righteous cry for help, the Lord hears and delivers them out of all their troubles." **Psalm 34:17**

I woke up with terrible vertigo, so dizzy I found myself stumbling most of the morning. For months I'd been trying to manage the MS flareups on my own, praying through the pain. Now, it was getting out of control, beyond me. To make matters worse, that morning I found Mom sitting on the edge of her bed crying. She said she'd been trying to get up and needed help but she couldn't remember my name. Trying to remain strong and calm, I told Mom, "Next time just yell out HELP!" And in that moment, I realized that's exactly what I needed to do for myself now, too.

November 5

"When I look at your heavens, the work of your fingers, the moon and the stars, which you have set in place, what is man that you are mindful of him, and the son of man that you care for him?" **Psalm 8:3-4**

A tornado swept through our area, damaging houses and touching down in our hometown Hughes Springs. I noticed that extreme weather and even solar changes affected both Mom and me with our neurological issues (Alzheimer's and MS). Once I recognized this, it helped me prepare for our diseases inside the house the same way I prepared vulnerable plants outside. I'm not sure what the correlation is, but perhaps the same way God gives us signs to prepare our homes and property for weather disasters, He does the same for our bodies and minds.

November 6

"Blessed are the merciful, for they shall receive mercy." **Matthew 5:7**

Mom had pneumonia again and her oxygen level was only 85. It was Heather's last visit before leaving for her new job; I told her I felt like a failure for not being able to stave off pneumonia again but no matter what I did or how hard I tried, nothing helped. Heather explained, with loving grace, that Mom had a deadly combination of COPD, Alzheimer's, and CHF and she was now in the final stages of COPD. She said even if Mom was in the hospital she would still be susceptible to pneumonia. That night I was on my knees praying; from what Heather told me, Mom's ending was near. I prayed for peace and grace, and no pain. I felt lighter when I finished praying. Praise Jesus.

November 7

"In this you rejoice, though now for a little while, if necessary, you have been grieved by various trials," **1 Peter: 1-6**

After my conversation with Nurse Heather the day before, I decided to start decorating for Christmas extra early. I wasn't sure how much time Mom had left and wanted all of us to have daily reminders of Jesus' birth. I put garland over the entryways and set up our vintage Christmas village, Mom's favorite. Then even though it was cold outside I got us some Andy's custard, wrapped Mom up in blankets and we ate on the patio.. We watched the orange and gold oak leaves floating down in the backyard and watched squirrels scampering with acorns along the fence. It was a lovely moment, something we both needed.

November 8

"He deprives of speech those who are trusted and takes away the discernment of the elders." **Job 12:20**

We were coloring together when Mom told me about her Aunt Juanita and those "evil daughters of hers up the hill". She was convinced one of the daughters was pictured in her new coloring book so she asked for scissors and defiantly cut it out.. Later she was carefully cleaning the scissors with Kleenex and said, "These scissors are the only thing I got when Aunt Juanita died. I had to steal them during the funeral from those evil girls." Lisa and I decided she was thinking of a "Little House" episode, along with the strong pneumonia antibiotic she was taking. We also hid the scissors that night. I thanked God that He was there to help and protect all of us.

November 9

Fear not, for I am with you; be not dismayed, for I am your God; I will strengthen you, I will help you, I will uphold you with my righteous right hand." **Isaiah 41:10**

I was in Tyler for an emergency neurology appointment where my doctor told me the MS was advancing. I had more lesions on my spinal cord along with extensive osteoporosis. After several tests, including watching me walk, she said I needed to be treated in the hospital. But I couldn't leave Mom that long, and I also couldn't take strong pain meds because I had to stay alert 24/7. So she arranged for me to have IV steroid treatments at home, still difficult but manageable with Lisa there. The entire drive home I prayed aloud for guidance. Life was never meant to be easy (read "Genesis") but with God, all things are possible. I had no fear.

November 10

"Answer me quickly, O Lord! My spirit fails! Hide not your face from me, lest I be like those who go down to the pit. Let me hear in the morning of your steadfast love, for in you I trust." **Psalm 143:7-8**

For the first time in years I was falling into despair. Between the pain of MS and caregiving I was struggling and unable to rest. Meanwhile one of Lisa's friends died so she was spending time away grieving. For Mom's sake, when Dad died (and many others in my life) I had to bury my grief, compartmentalize. I remained in scripture and prayed every moment I could. Even in my despair, I knew I was never alone. I was happy Lisa was able to externalize emotional pain, and eventually I would learn to do that, too. For now, it remained internal and only God could heal my broken parts.

November 11

"Only take care, and keep your soul diligently, lest you forget the things that your eyes have seen, and lest they depart from your heart all the days of your life. Make them known to your children and your children's children—" **Deuteronomy 4:9**

And then, a little miracle: I got to babysit my grandbaby for the first time and that completely lifted me from all the darkness. Jason also asked me to decorate their Christmas tree for them so while the baby slept I made the small tree extra sparkly and bright. I changed and fed my grandson, and when he fussed I sang what was once Jason's favorite lullaby, "Stay Awake" from Mary Poppins. He fell asleep in my arms, and that's where he stayed until they got home. I prayed endless love and gratitude over that little boy, then and now.

November 12

"Behold, I send an angel before you to guard you on the way and to bring you to the place that I have prepared.." **Exodus 23:20**

The sun was up but Mom was still sleeping so I decided to set up our Christmas angel in the yard. It was cold and by the time I got everything out of the shed it started sprinkling. Regardless, I was determined to place that angel. After hooking up all the extension cords and hammering stakes in the ground to make her stand up, I plugged it in. It was raining hard now and I was drenched but happy. The angel, covered in gold lights, shone brightly in front of the dining room window so Mom could see it at breakfast. Another new season was approaching; I knew God was guarding us, and our Christmas angel was a lovely representative.

November 13

"For this reason I bow my knees before the Father, from whom every family in heaven and on earth is named," **Ephesians 3:14-15**

Lisa and I were both stressed and for the first time we were snapping at each other. I was exhausted; my upcoming steroid treatments would help but until then, I was in constant pain. Lisa was tired from her very stressful job and felt guilty that she couldn't be home more to help. But mostly, Mom wasn't remembering who we were anymore; she was lost and confused about everything. We knew we wouldn't have her much longer so my prayers were that Lisa and I would remain strong and united, and not allow darkness to come between us. Too many families crumble when times get hardest but with God leading the way, we would survive.

November 14

"O Lord, you are my God; I will exalt you; I will praise your name, for you have done wonderful things, plans formed of old, faithful and sure."
Isaiah 25:1

Hospice came early. Mom had fever which explained why she was out of breath even just being lifted in and out of her wheelchair. She stayed in bed later than usual and called out for me, "Ann-Marie, Ann-Marie!" As always I ran full-speed, grateful she remembered my name. "I'm hungry," she said. I moved her to her rocking chair and turned on the Christmas globe she'd seen many times before. "Oh how beautiful!", clapping her hands like a little girl. Sometimes with Alzheimer's, God's grace is in the gift of rediscovery. Almost every time she saw anything now it was all brand new....

November 15

"Even youths shall faint and be weary, and young men shall fall exhausted;" **Isaiah 40:30**

When hospice arrived to give Mom a shower I told the nurse how she'd changed and was almost peaceful now. But of course the opposite happened. Mom started raging about the "bad guy" who was coming to steal her money and clothes. Throughout the shower she yelled at the poor nurse. "Why are you doing this to me? I want out! Get me out of here!" I tried to help but Mom was in a complete frenzy, wheezing, and grinding her teeth. Finally, after drying her off the nurse rubbed lotion on Mom's legs. She 'came back', joking and happy. She was fine but I was not. I prayed for strength to keep going because I just didn't have a choice.

November 16

"For God alone, O my soul, wait in silence, for my hope is from him."
Psalm 62:5

Every year my "Honeybee" friends Betsy, Amy, Paula and I go to Carmella's, a beautiful drive-thru Christmas light display but for the first time I wanted to back out. I wasn't sure what to say or how to talk anymore, and worried about what might happen when I left. But after praying about it, I went. They were all Mom's former students and loved her, too, so I was surprised they only briefly asked about her. I think they didn't want to push me to talk so I mostly stayed silent, which was painful. I knew they cared, but at the time it was very difficult to be around almost anyone other than Lisa. It felt like we were in the middle of a war and it was hard to relate to anyone who wasn't in it.

November 17

"Are they not all ministering spirits sent out to serve for the sake of those who are to inherit salvation?" **Hebrews 1:14**

The hospice nurse was concerned about Mom's swollen feet; she said it could be from congestive heart failure and/or not elevating enough. She said the COPD was getting worse and her oxygen levels were dropping, too. That day Mom was slumped over in her rocking chair holding her purse with the 3 little animals inside. She hadn't carried a purse in years, but now it was 'packed' as if she was leaving. The night before she talked about going to supper with "the beautiful woman in white". When I told the nurse about it she got chills and said, "I hear that a lot near the end; they start packing instinctively, knowing they're going someplace, or talking to loved ones…"

November 18

"Or do you not know that your body is a temple of the Holy Spirit within you, whom you have from God? You are not your own," **1 Corinthians 6:19**

Lisa called out for me while she was changing Mom into her pajamas. Mom, talking in 3rd person, told me, "She shouldn't have these on," motioning towards the cartoon gnome pajamas she'd worn many times before. I felt something important was happening. "No, of course not," I said, and brought her a pretty floral nightgown. I asked if this was better and she nodded. Then, for the first time in months, she wanted to wash her face. I carefully brushed her hair and helped her to bed. I prayed for understanding, but I believe God made Mom aware that she needed to be dressed in something more dignified for this holy time of her life...

November 19

"For it is written, "'He will command his angels concerning you, to guard you,'" **Luke 4:10**

I woke up at 3 a.m. expecting to help Mom but she never stirred. When the sun came up she still wasn't awake. I listened to the monitor and couldn't hear breathing or movement so I texted Lisa. For the first time, I was afraid to go into Mom's room alone so we went in together. Her breathing was shallow. By 8 a.m. she was sitting up, wheezing and saying her chest hurt. After taking her to the bathroom she wanted to go back to bed, something she'd never done before. She was asleep before I left her room. I thought of the angel outside and knew I needed to move it. It was freezing but, with tears flowing, I moved it directly in front of Mom's bay window. Jesus, and now our Christmas angel, were watching over Mom.

November 20

"A Psalm of David, when he was in the wilderness of Judah. O God, you are my God; earnestly I seek you; my soul thirsts for you; my flesh faints for you, as in a dry and weary land where there is no water." **Psalm 63:1**

It was the third and final day of steroid infusions and my head was pounding. I usually got migraines after one infusion but now, after two in a row with another to go, my head felt like a giant parade balloon. I was taking care of Mom while waiting for my nurse to arrive and while trying to help her into the wheelchair she slipped out of my hands. I was too weak to hold her up; the IV needle was still in my arm for the steroids. I had to wake Lisa and she called the fire department; they helped Mom and thankfully she was fine, but I wasn't. Only God could help us all now.

November 21

"Light is sown for the righteous, and joy for the upright in heart." **Psalm 97:11**

In the midst of everything, Lisa and I were determined to have a combination Thanksgiving and birthday feast for Mom and our family. Her 85th birthday was on the 25th; we knew it would be her last so we wanted to make it special. I was amped up on steroids so I prepped all the food and then cleaned and scrubbed the house, inside and out. I finally stopped to watch two movies with Mom: *The Bishop's Wife* which she loved, and a new version of *Dr. Dolittle*. For the first time in weeks she laughed loudly when she saw a dolphin wearing a top hat. I cried, thanking Jesus that I could hear her laughter again; it had been too long. I didn't know, but it would also be the last time.

.

November 22

"He gives strength to the weary and increases the power of the weak."
Isaiah 40:29

Around 3 a.m. I helped Mom to the bathroom. She didn't have to call me to help anymore, I just came as soon as I heard her. She was struggling to breathe, beginning to panic, so I put the oxygen tubes back in her nose and rubbed her head to help calm her. "Am I dying?" she asked, frightened. "No Mom, you'll be fine, just relax and try to go back to sleep. I love you." I went back to my room but couldn't sleep so with renewed strength from God (and steroids), I got out the ladder and put icicle Christmas lights in the trees outside. Later while Mom was eating lunch, I moved her bed to the center of her room so Lisa and I could both sit next to her. This needed to happen more than I realized.

November 23

"And everyone who lives and believes in me shall never die. Do you believe this?" **John 11:26**

It was the day before Thanksgiving and Mom was becoming delirious, wanting to go to the bathroom for no reason every few hours to the point of exhaustion. The hospice nurse said it was like an "end game battle" between Alzheimer's and COPD, the first causing restlessness and anxiety, the other depleting her lungs. Both diseases were wearing her out. She gave Mom a shower but even having her hair brushed didn't calm her like before. That night Lisa was so worried she stayed with Mom all night. I listened on the monitor as Mom sleep-talked for hours, nonsensical, just like Dad and Grandma Birdie Lee at the end of their lives. I prayed Mom would get better but I knew. I knew.

November 24

"Give thanks in all circumstances; for this is the will of God in Christ Jesus for you." **1 Thessalonians 5:18**

Lisa and I were weary, but at 7 a.m. we started cooking for Thanksgiving. For the first time ever, Mom didn't get up but she'd been so restless this week we let her sleep. Everyone arrived at 1pm. Mom was still sleeping so we decided to go ahead and eat. Everyone filled their plates but moments after I said the Thanksgiving prayer, our world fell apart. Both Mom and the baby needed help. After that the food was cold so we wrapped it all up in to-go boxes. Mom never got up; she hadn't eaten since early the day before. Lisa and I prayed; we decided to call hospice the next day, at least someone deserved a happy Thanksgiving day. As for Lisa and me, it was time to really pray.

November 25

"Or do you not know that your body is a temple of the Holy Spirit within you, whom you have from God? You are not your own," **1 Corinthians 6:19**

This was Mom's 85th birthday. After sleeping most of the day before and unable to wake her now, we called hospice. Her vitals were dropping. Every now and then she'd rally, incoherently saying she needed to use the bathroom, then she'd fade away again. After 2 p.m. her breathing changed. She didn't open her eyes anymore. At 5:30 I called Lisa at her office to come home. Mom was leaving soon and I didn't want her to miss anything. On my knees, I prayed. I had no idea what to do at this point, but God did.

November 26

"Be gracious to me, O Lord, for I am in distress; my eye is wasted from grief; my soul and my body also." **Psalm 31:9**

From 2 a.m. to almost 5 a.m. my crazy nesting issues kicked in due to the steroids. I prayed continuously as I quietly collected things that I knew would hurt Lisa and me in the future. I bagged up Mom's giant pill holder and flushed all the meds she would never need again. I organized things to donate or give away, including Mom's books and rocks. I moved the living room furniture back in place, no longer needing wheelchair access. Later, Jason, Mimi, and the baby came over to say their goodbyes and so did our cousins Preston and Cliff. Mom opened her eyes a little during the day, and then she was gone again. It was a strange, sad day, but Jesus helped us through it all.

November 27

"And he said, "Behold, I see the heavens opened, and the Son of Man standing at the right hand of God." **Acts 7:56**

After being completely unresponsive for four days, a miracle. Mom opened her eyes, looked directly at Lisa and me, and smiled. She reached for our hands and kissed them with a look of absolute bliss on her face. We were stunned. Then she sort of backed out of our world and began air-kissing others, joyfully smiling at them, looking happier than we'd ever seen her. Lisa said she looked 'serene'. Then she was gone again, sleeping peacefully. It was wonderful to know that Mom was on her way to Jesus, and we were blessed to have gotten a glimpse of her joy in advance.

November 28

"Commit your way to the Lord; trust in him, and he will act." **Psalm 37:5**

All night and morning Mom was sleep-coughing. It was wet sounding, like the worst type of pneumonia. I waited until morning to call hospice and after describing what was happening, the nurse said she'd come over after a staff meeting later that morning. I was furious. This moment with Mom was the entire reason for having hospice. I told her not to come at all and fired her. I was crying, angry, and grieving with zero sleep. Desperately, I prayed for help and instantly pictured Nurse Heather. She was with another hospice company but I called her anyway. She gave me advice and then she called Nurse Leslie. Both of those God-gifted nurses came over immediately to help, praise Jesus.

November 29

"Lord, listen to me and answer me. I am poor and helpless." **Psalm 86:1**

The fluid in Mom's lungs sounded like an old-fashioned vaporizing machine next to a loudspeaker. That's the only way to describe it, like nothing I'd ever heard in a human. Sometimes she would suddenly burst out a terrifyingly loud cough. It didn't seem to bother Lisa but it was the first time I was unnerved. After 5 or 6 hours of this I had to leave the room to pray for strength to get through it all. I came back in the room with earplugs; it helped. He helped.

November 30

"For I consider that the sufferings of this present time are not worth comparing with the glory that is to be revealed to us." **Romans 8:18**

Through everything, Mom's face remained peaceful, never showing any signs of discomfort or pain. The room was cold; the ceiling fan had to be on for circulation so I bundled up in the faux leopard fur coat Mom loved to wear. I was proud of Lisa during those last days and nights; she stayed calm when I couldn't. We were, and are, a really great team. Lisa is a wonderful sister and I pray for siblings who don't get along, especially during the death of a loved one. No one else in life can share that type of grief with you.

December

"By this all people will know that you are my disciples, if you have love for one another."
John 13:34-35

December 1

"I thank my God in all my remembrance of you, always in every prayer of mine for you all making my prayer with joy, because of your partnership in the gospel from the first day until now." **Philippians 1:3-5**

Mom had been transitioning 8 days now. All we could do was keep her clean and give her medication as needed. Nurse Leslie was with us in the end, helping us all hours of the day and night, and Heather visited, too. But mostly it was just Lisa and me keeping watch over our mother, making sure she was comfortable and pain-free. Her breathing was still loud, but not unbearable anymore. At her bedside, Lisa and I shared stories of when she was our funny and quirky mother and teacher. We stayed next to her praying day and night, both of us holding her hands.

December 2

"Can a mother forget the baby at her breast and have no compassion on the child she has borne? Though she may forget, I will not forget you! See, I have engraved you on the palms of my hands; your walls are ever before me." **Isaiah 49:15-16**

Mom died on 12-02-22 at 2:02 p.m. Before leaving she'd forgotten almost everything about her life: our father Jerry, our stepfather Gene, 43+ years teaching high school, how to read and write, colors, food. But at the very end, even though she forgot Lisa and me, she always knew Jesus. She was cared for with never-ending sources of love. We honored our mother and father to the end of their lives, to the best of our abilities. Thank you, dear Jesus, for such a gift.

December 3

"He will wipe away every tear from their eyes, and death shall be no more, neither shall there be mourning, nor crying, nor pain anymore, for the former things have passed away." **Revelation 21:4**

After almost 5 years, I was no longer a caregiver. From this day in 2022 until mid-January 2023 my journal was completely blank. Even now, I remember the loss I felt, not knowing where to go from that point on. In the last year of Mom's life I rarely left the house; she thrived on routine and it threw her into a tailspin when I wasn't there. So I stayed with her, answering all her needs from early morning to night. I didn't do it out of guilt or a sense of atonement, I did it to honor God and His blessings. I miss her and appreciate every lesson I learned, even the heartbreaking ones.

December 4

"O Lord, you are my God; I will exalt you; I will praise your name, for you have done wonderful things, plans formed of old, faithful and sure."
Isaiah 25:1

Even a year later I sometimes struggled integrating back into society. My first big step was going to church and getting involved with a wonderful Life Group class, but I was still ordering groceries to be delivered instead of shopping myself. So to completely shake up my life, I went on a tour of Italy. It was glorious, life-changing, and gave me the jump-start I needed to very literally reenter the world. I was in prayer almost every moment, thanking God for such an opportunity and for restoring my life again.

December 5

"Blessed are you who are hungry now, for you shall be satisfied. "Blessed are you who weep now, for you shall laugh." **Luke 6:21**

Betsy, Paula, Amy and I were getting together for our 4th annual trip to see Carmella's drive-thru Christmas lights. After sharing a wonderful meal, we drove through the beautiful lights and then did the walking tour in the freezing cold, laughing all the way. On the way home we stopped at local Shiver's for hot chocolate, another tradition for us. I gave them the engraved leather pen holders that I bought in Italy and in turn, they shared happy stories about Mom, aka "Mrs. Brown" from our high school years. I thank God for my friends and pray everyone has people they can turn to through every crisis and celebration in life.

December 6

"A Psalm for giving thanks. Make a joyful noise to the Lord, all the earth! Serve the Lord with gladness! Come into his presence with singing!"
Psalm 100:1-2

It was a lovely night at the Longview Symphony Christmas concert, a new tradition for our entire family. During the sing-along portion Lisa and I laughed when we both realized that if Mom were there her voice would be louder than anyone around us. Mom loved to sing and she did so to the very end of her life. My sister and I cried and hugged as we sang together, in joyful remembrance of our wonderful mother.

December 7

"But the Lord is faithful. He will establish you and guard you against the evil one." **Romans 12:15**

Mom loved Facebook and spent hours communicating with her former students. Near the end of her computer days she forgot how to login to her account so I often received new friend requests from her. One day recently I received another friend request from "Mom", or rather a monster who hacked her account. It was daunting seeing her name and picture there, especially this time of year. Before reporting and blocking the hacker, I knew it wouldn't matter but I sent him a message saying I was her daughter and that she died a year ago. I also said I'd pray for their soul for hurting me in such a way…

December 8

"Rejoice with those who rejoice, weep with those who weep." **Romans 12:15**

More than a year later I was appreciative when people remembered that Lisa and I were still grieving. My friends Michael and Sharon Ingmire sent us a beautiful Christmas bell ornament engraved in remembrance; it will forever hang on our Christmas tree. Dr. Fred Eichelman, Francine Locke and Jim and Brenda Woody gave us remembrances, too. Funerals are a wonderful time to catch up with family and friends but it's the quiet times, even years later, when you sometimes need your friends the most.

December 9

"Behold, children are a heritage from the Lord, the fruit of the womb a reward." **Psalm 127:3**

I got to babysit my grandson while Jason and Mimi attended a Christmas party. It was wonderful to spend time with the little guy on my own, holding him and singing 'Stay Awake' ten or more times. When he finally fell asleep I tried putting him in his crib but he woke up and cried longer than I could stand. I went back to check on him and he grabbed my hand, holding it to his chest as he curled up around it. I realized all he wanted was someone there with him as he fell asleep. I stayed until he was snoring. He was born 3 months before Mom died and I thanked God for giving me the caregiving skills and instincts needed not only for my parents, but now for my beautiful baby grandson.

December 10

"Finally, all of you, have unity of mind, sympathy, brotherly love, a tender heart, and a humble mind." **1 Peter 3:8**

I was invited to a Christmas party where I wouldn't know many people and I was almost frozen with anxiety. Most of my friends wouldn't understand this because I was once a national speaker, sometimes appearing in front of thousands of people and I never got nervous. Now, I was on the verge of backing out, trying to come up with any excuse not to go. Instead I got on my knees and prayed about it. I prayed for the fears to go away and for God to teach me how to communicate and interact again. I went to the party and although it was difficult at times, I had fun. Praise God.

December 11

"But let him ask in faith, with no doubting, for the one who doubts is like a wave of the sea that is driven and tossed by the wind." **James 1:6**

I called Lisa because I was spiraling with too many "what ifs". What if I was on the wrong path when I moved to Texas? What if Mom and Dad would've been better off with someone else helping them? Lisa, always the calm voice of reason, reminded me that I saved them from their black mold-filled house; she couldn't have managed that alone. Jason and Mimi never would've moved to Texas where they were now thriving and had a baby. And she reminded me that from the start, I followed Jesus' guidance, not my own. Thank you, God for my sister. Amen.

December 12

Keep your life free from love of money, and be content with what you have, for he has said, "I will never leave you nor forsake you." **Hebrews 13:5**

When I moved to Texas I brought my very fancy convertible car with me. It was fun to drive with the top down in California, not so much in Texas with ultra-hot summers and freezing cold winters. Plus with no backseat it wasn't grandson-friendly, so I decided to sell it. As I signed the paperwork I realized that car was the last material thing I had from my decades in California. I never missed my old life because I was so busy with the new one, but with more time on my hands, would that change? Driving home in my "normal" car, I prayed for peace and then smiled and thanked Him as I realized He'd already given it to me.

December 13

"With all humility and gentleness, with patience, bearing with one another in love," **Ephesians 4:2**

After much prayer and discussions, Lisa moved into a rental house and Jason, Mimi, the baby and their two dogs moved in with me. It was a big adjustment at first; after years of living in mostly silence, my house was now sometimes completely chaotic with dogs barking, the baby crying, and people coming and going all the time. But oh, what a blessing God had given all of us! I was now able to see my grandson (and soon a second one) grow up. We prayed during our family meals at the dining table again, and Lisa came over almost daily. Our home was full of love and laughter, and Jesus was with us all. Hallelujah!

December 14

"I thank my God in all my remembrance of you, always in every prayer of mine for you all making my prayer with joy, because of your partnership in the gospel from the first day until now." **Philippians 1: 3-5**

The baby monitor in the baby's nursery brought back memories of waking up in the middle of the night to help Mom. Even two years later I still sometimes woke at 3 a.m., that 'magic hour' when I'd hear her stirring in her room. A few months before she died Mom helped me decorate our guest/nursery room with peel-on wall stickers. It was another big adjustment when I had to remove those stickers because the baby was now in Mom's old room. But this house will forever hold so many reminders of her, and I can only imagine how magnificent her new Home is now.

December 15

"With all humility and gentleness, with patience, bearing with one another in love," **Ephesians 4:2**

The only bad thing about living with a young family is illness. Almost every other week one, or all of us, were sick. In a way that's when I thrived and my caregiving abilities kicked in, from spending hours in the ER to making unending pots of homemade soup. At one point everyone had Covid except me; even the baby was sick. I worked day and night doing whatever I could to help and comfort my family. And all the while, I expressed gratitude to God for teaching me skills I never would've learned if I'd stayed in California.

December 16

"And my God will supply every need of yours according to his riches in glory in Christ Jesus." **Philippians 4:19**

Lisa was always a wonderful person but as "Aunt Lisa" she somehow managed to become even better. She loves my grandson almost as much as I do and visits every chance she gets. She's always armed with several new toys and when she can't come over she sends funny videos of her singing songs or acting silly. He loves her, too, and runs to the door hopping up and down when he sees her red car drive up. What a blessing this child has been for all of us, and later his little brother, too.

December 17

"You shall not see your brother's donkey or his ox fallen down by the way and ignore them. You shall help him to lift them up again."
Deuteronomy 22:4

Writing and journaling was my main source of escape during the caregiving years. I often shared my 'Mom stories' on social media, especially when that illuminated the ways God was working through us. As a result I received hundreds of messages and texts from people asking advice about their own elderly family member. I always prayed before answering because while I'll never be the definitive "expert" on caregiving, I can honestly say that Jesus Christ had a major part in every decision I made. Allowing God to guide is the best and most any of us can do when caring for a loved one.

December 18

"But he said to me, "My grace is sufficient for you, for my power is made perfect in weakness." Therefore I will boast all the more gladly of my weaknesses, so that the power of Christ may rest upon me." **2 Corinthians 12:9**

In 2024 after almost a full year of unending upper respiratory illnesses, I was diagnosed with 'mild COPD'. The same month after a battery of testing I was also diagnosed with Mild Cognitive Impairment, aka Early Onset Alzheimer's. Because of Mom's ending, this could have been devastating news. But with the help and support of my family, friends, and church, I'm refusing these diseases in the name of Jesus Christ. At the same time, I've learned that, like Paul, sometimes humans have to suffer in order to remain close to God. Either way, I'm happy and unafraid. God is here and I will praise Him forever, in sickness and health.

December 19

"And thus you shall greet him: 'Peace be to you, and peace be to your house, and peace be to all that you have." **1 Samuel 25:6**

When I first found my house with Mom we both knew it was a blessing. There was a large bedroom with a separate entrance for Lisa and Mom's room had a large window seat for displaying her rocks. My room had a large bathroom with a jacuzzi tub, exactly what I needed for sore and tired bones. The beautiful fenced-in backyard was shaded with tall oak trees and full of flourishing plants and flowers. And especially for Mom, rock gardens were scattered all around the front and backyards But as great as this house was for Mom, it was even better for Jason, Mimi and, eventually, two little boys. I know Mom would be even happier to see it now.

December 20

"For we are glad when we are weak and you are strong. Your restoration is what we pray for." **2 Corinthians 13**

My grandson had a high fever and after an ER visit we were told he'd need to be quarantined. There was now a newborn in the house and Mimi needed to stay with him, and Jason worked full-time and couldn't stay home. So I was in full-blown caregiving mode again with the little guy, but I have to admit, it was fun cuddling up and watching 'Rudolph' on TV with him. It had been a very long time since I'd taken care of a sick child on my own. As he held onto my arm, sniffling and coughing, I prayed and cried a little, overwhelmed with happiness and gratitude for my little grandson.

December 21

"I have said these things to you, that in me you may have peace. In the world you will have tribulation. But take heart; I have overcome the world."
John 16:33

I had my grandson all day and into the evening. His throat hurt so we made a smoothie together (his choice of ingredients). He only drank a little of it and then napped in my room, snoring. When he woke up he curled up in my lap and slept some more. He never ate, barely drank, and I just prayed for healing, stroking his hair. I knew he'd be fine; children are resilient. But what I've learned is that the hardest part of human suffering is usually someone else watching helplessly. And speaking of suffering, I now had bronchitis again and had to pray for healing for myself ...

December 22

"Bless the Lord, O my soul, and forget not all his benefits, who forgives all your iniquity, who heals all your diseases, who redeems your life from the pit, who crowns you with steadfast love and mercy," **Psalm 103:2-4**

Just as my grandson was getting better, I was now getting worse. I could tell it was in my lower lungs and I was now taking the same nebulizer breathing treatments and medications I'd given Mom for her COPD. It was almost Christmas and I had already missed most of the church services, either caring for my sick family or being sick myself. I prayed to keep the fear of COPD out of my mind, but thoughts of Mom's death kept lurking around. My cough sounded so familiar, just like Mom. I prayed fervently, and so did my friends and family.

December 23

"The Lord sustains him on his sickbed; in his illness you restore him to full health." **Psalm 41:3**

Everyone left for the day to shop so even though I was sick, I wanted to clean the house for Christmas Eve. I straightened the living room, did laundry, and swept the leaves off the patio. By the time I finished I needed to get back in bed. One of my biggest problems is knowing when to keep going and when to stop and "be still". And for now, being still was more important than cleaning the house, even if it was for Jesus' birthday.

December 24

"And the Word became flesh and dwelt among us, and we have seen his glory, glory as of the only Son from the Father, full of grace and truth."
John 1:14

I'm someone who wants to decorate for Christmas the moment October is finished. I like to celebrate Christ's entry into this world as long as possible, so it was devastating when I was too sick to attend our Christmas Eve church service. I was almost too weak to do much more than help fill a few stockings before going back to bed. My fever was high; I was sure I had pneumonia. But I still found joy in my heart as I gave thanks for Jesus' birth and life, and the life and light He brought to all of us. Sick or not.

December 25

"For unto you is born this day in the city of David a Savior, who is Christ the Lord." **Luke 2:11**

It was a beautiful Christmas morning. My grandsons were blessed with toys and surprises, and Lisa was with us as we opened presents, laughing and having fun. We had lunch together, celebrating the birth of Jesus all afternoon. Then, as soon as Lisa went home and the kids were napping, I drove myself to the ER. As I suspected, I had pneumonia. I was given a prescription for antibiotics and after picking them up, I went to bed to isolate. I prayed for healing, but knew at this point I had a long road of sickness ahead of me.

December 26

"Iron sharpens iron, and one man sharpens another." **Proverbs 27:17**

Lisa was sick, too, with bronchitis; between the two of us we were a mess. I prayed for her, upset that I couldn't be there to help her and she felt the same about me. Even though Lisa and I had sadness and difficulties with Mom, there was also abundant laughter and happy times together. We learned more about life and death those last two years than ever before. For now, we had to rely on texting to check on each other. God blessed me enormously when He chose Lisa as my sister.

December 27

"Heal me, O Lord, and I shall be healed; save me, and I shall be saved, for you are my praise." **Jeremiah 17:14**

I was coughing so hard I tore a ligament at the bottom of my rib cage. Because of Mom I knew that even with fractured ribs there's nothing anyone can do about it other than use ice packs and wait for it to heal. But it now hurt to cough, which was dangerous with pneumonia because coughing and antibiotics are the only way to get better. I used every homeopathic remedy I could find, and as always, I prayed, along with my wonderful Gage Life group at church.

December 28

"Do not be anxious about anything, but in everything by prayer and supplication with thanksgiving let your requests be made known to God. And the peace of God, which surpasses all understanding, will guard your hearts and your minds in Christ Jesus.." **Philippians 4:6-7**

We were under a tornado watch; rain was pouring with lightning striking all around. In the midst of it, my church friend Wendy Sherman came to the house to deliver a bottle of castor oil. She'd been texting me about all the benefits, including helping heal broken bones. That night I slathered the stuff all over my rib cage and topped it with my ice pack. It actually seemed to help; after an hour some of the pain was gone. It still hurt to cough, but not as much. The Lord provides us with all we need, including friends like Wendy.

December 29

"Have I not commanded you? Be strong and courageous. Do not be frightened, and do not be dismayed, for the Lord your God is with you wherever you go."" **Joshua 1:9**

Around 2 a.m. I had another coughing fit and felt a rip again in the same place under my ribs. I slathered on more castor oil and using a long-sleeved t-shirt, I rigged a sling-type device that held the ice pack in place. The pneumonia seemed to be getting worse, causing my back to ache and MS to flare up. And still, I felt strong inside, continually praying, thanking God for my blessings. I felt sure I would get better, but even if I didn't I thanked Him even more. What a wonderful life and family He's given me. Even one more breath is more than I deserve, but I'll keep taking as many as He allows.

December 30

"Come now, you who say, "Today or tomorrow we will go into such and such a town and spend a year there and trade and make a profit"— yet you do not know what tomorrow will bring. What is your life? For you are a mist that appears for a little time and then vanishes. Instead you ought to say, "If the Lord wills, we will live and do this or that." **James 4:13-15**

Pneumonia forced me to be still and pray hard about my life. I realized I needed to make sure my house was in order, something I often advised others to do. Because of this, I also realized it was time to get my book published, along with this devotional. If I could help make anyone's caregiving life easier, or in the least avoid some of my pitfalls and mistakes, I needed to do so. And with God's help, as soon as I could get out of bed again, I would.

December 31

"And let us not grow weary of doing good, for in due season we will reap, if we do not give up." **Galatians 6:9**

My journal for 2024 journal ended on New Year's Eve because I was too sick to write anymore. At my family's strong encouragement, I went back to the ER. I was checked into the hospital in critical condition with double pneumonia where I stayed almost 2 weeks. In a full-circle moment, I was now thanking Jesus for giving me such wonderful caregivers, including family and friends who love me. And I am praying this right now for anyone reading today: God bless and keep you, and if you are a caregiver I pray God will give you strength, patience, discernment, kindness and love that only He can bring in abundance. And keep praying, He is listening and He is there for you!

‘